# HeartCare Healthy Lifestyle Recipes

### 4th edition 2003

### Compiled by N E Sanderson.

**Please visit our web site - www.heartcarecsg.co.uk**

Copyright remains with HeartCare Cardiac Support Group and N E Sanderson

Publisher: - Neville E Sanderson

Date publication of fourth edition: - 2003

ISBN: - 0 9530810 1 X

Printed by: -

DTP: - Amber Graphics, 25 Willow Road, Lowestoft, NR33 7BJ
(A division of N E Sanderson & Co.)

I would like to thank the following for all the help and encouragement given in compiling this book: -

My wife, Margaret;
my daughter Jayne and her husband Steve;
HeartCare Committee members, in particular Willy Rix, our Secretary;
Pat Harris for help with the typing; and
Rachel Biggins for her hard work in checking these recipes for their suitability for CHD patients. Rachel has very kindly done this for us free of all charges.
This is very much appreciated

This fourth edition of *"Healthy Lifestyle"* recipes has been published using equipment purchased with the help of a grant from the National Lotteries Charities Board.

Dear Neville        June 2003

I will not be charging a fee for the work I have done.

There is a point I would like to make about the use of fats and oils. The problem with oils is their chemical structure and the damage they can undergo in the cooking process. This is why we recommend extra virgin olive oil because it is stable even at high temperatures because of its chemical bonds.

You have no doubt heard about the essential fats omega 3 and omega 6 that we need in our diets. These are found in oily fish such as salmon, trout, mackerel, tuna, sardine and herring and are needed for good heart health and many nuts and seeds. The fats found in margarine that in the ingredients are classed as hydrogenated and many deep friend foods such as chips are chemically altered in a way that can block the absorption of these essential fats we need for the healthy structure of the cell walls found in our brains and arteries.

Trans fatty acids occur when any unsaturated oil is heated for a long period as in deep frying. They also form the hydrogenation process used in making margarine, shortening and other products. Anything, therefore, that contains partially hydrogenated fat contains trans fatty acids. Deep fried foods contain an abundance as do many pre-packaged foods. Trans fats block many of the good functions that essential fats have.

It is important not to become **"fat phobic"** but **"fat smart"**.

Cook with extra virgin olive oil.

Think if you really need a spread on your bread - a lot of times such as if we are eating peanut butter we don't. The Italians dip their bread into olive oil. Find a non-hydrogenated oil margarine from your Health Food shop. But I wouldn't cook with it. Essential fats such as the Omega 3s and Omega 6s can be found in Flax seed oil, extra virgin sunflower oil, walnut oil etc. All these can be got from your Health Food shop and are very different from the oils you get in a supermarket. They are good for your cell membranes making them nice and bendy, not hard and compact. Use them on salads, baked potatoes or drizzled on vegetables. They do you good.

Anyway, good luck with the book Neville and I hope this has been of some help.

Yours sincerely
Rachel Biggins
Nutritional Consultant, DipION; Diridol; BANT regd.

*(British Association of Nutritional Therapists (BANT) is the association of Nutritional Therapists that only accepts members from quality colleges with suitable experience.*
*If you think you could benefit from a one-to-one Nutritional consultation then you can find a local nutritionist by phoning 0870 606 1284 or accessing their web site at www.bant.org.uk)*

HeartCare Healthy Lifestyle Recipes - fourth edition - 2003

# *Contents*

| | Page No. |
|---|---|
| The Nutritional Consultancy | 5 |
| Aims and Objectives | 7 |
| Introduction | 8 |
| Healthy Eating Hints | 8 |
| Adapting Your Own Recipes | 9 |
| Five a Day | 10 |
| Vitamins | 10 |
| Conversion Charts | 11 |
| Starters | 12 |
| Soups | 16 |
| Salads | 23 |
| Herbs and Spices | 29 |
| Fish | 64 |
| Main Courses | 75 |
| Desserts | 100 |
| Index | 114 |

**Please visit our web site - www.heartcarecsg.co.uk**

HeartCare Healthy Lifestyle Recipes - fourth edition - 2003

## *HeartCare's Aims and Objectives*

The Association is established to relieve sickness and distress among persons who are suffering or who have suffered from heart disease and the families of such persons.

To educate the above persons and the public in all matters concerning heart disease.

In furtherance of the above aims but not further or otherwise the Association shall have the following powers: -

a) To promote the welfare of cardiac patients both at home and in hospital.

b) To promote and provide support and aftercare for patients and their families/carers when resuming home and social life.

c) To establish and facilitate local contact, support and counselling services accessible to anyone with a heart complaint, their families and friends.

d) To increase public awareness of heart disease, its causes, treatment, implications and help available.

e) To liaise with existing groups in this or similar fields

f) To act as an information centre for those people requiring literature on heart disease.

g) To facilitate meetings among heart disease sufferers and their families and those persons who understand their needs and problems. To exchange information and experiences relating to Coronary Heart Disease.

**Please visit our web site - www.heartcarecsg.co.uk**

## *Introduction*

All the recipes in this book have been chosen for healthy eating and have been adapted by using leaner meats, no cream or butter, less oil, less or no eggs and less or low-fat cheeses. These recipes are low in fat and high in fibre. All have been checked by Rachel Biggins, Nutritional Consultant. See her letter on page 5.
We hope you will enjoy trying these recipes.

All proceeds from the sale of this recipe book will go directly to HeartCare for the development of projects.
No administrative charge is made.

## *HeartCare Healthy Eating Hints*

A few adjustments to the way we cook, can make a difference to the fat content of our food.
Avoid frying - it is better to grill, microwave, steam or bake food with the minimum of oil.
Do not use lard or meat fats. You can use poly/mono unsaturated as an alternative, but Virgin Olive Oil is best
Stews and soups can be cooked in advance. When cool, the fat rises to the surface and can be skimmed off with a spoon.
Use low fat live yoghurt as a low calorie dressing for salads or substitute oil based dressings on salads with a lemon juice and herb dressing (See recipe).
Try using flax oil which is rich in omega 3s or virgin olive oil.
Try sorbets, low fat frozen yoghurt or lower fat ice creams, as an occasional topping on fruit.
With chicken portions or fish portions, you could coat the portions with low fat live yoghurt then dip in breadcrumbs, grill or oven cook, **do not fry.** This is much healthier than the usual egg and breadcrumb mix and tastes as if it has been fried.
Spray cans of vegetable/olive oil are available and they use very small amounts of oil. You can get refillable ones.
Cut the fat off meats and take the skin off chicken before cooking, this reduces the fat content greatly.
Instead of adding cream to soups and casseroles, mix together one tablespoon of corn-flour with three tablespoons of cold water and add as a thickener. Alternatively you can use live yoghurt.
Try skimmed milk in recipes and sauces or as a drink. It is low in fat and contains more calcium than other milks. Soya milk is also useful, high in proteins, low fat and beneficial for menopausal ladies.
Pan fry minced beef or lamb and pour off excess fat, or allow to cool and skim the fat off the top.
Try low fat Cheddar type cheese, Edam or low fat cottage cheese.
Honey is a very good substitute for sugar - try it as a replacement.

HeartCare Healthy Lifestyle Recipes - fourth edition - 2003

# *HeartCare Healthy Lifestyles Recipes*

## *The Basic Rules for Eating for a Healthy Heart are: -*

1. Eat more foods rich in carbohydrates, particularly bread, rice, fruit and vegetables and pasta.
2. Reduce the amount of salt and sugar
3. Eat less fat, particularly saturated fat
4. Maintain an ideal body weight.

### *Adapting Your Own Recipes*

It is possible to adapt your own favourite recipes so that they are lower in saturated fat by using less oil and less high fat food than those stated in the recipe.

Cream is replaced with low fat fromage frais.

The use of herbs will improve the flavour of many low-fat recipes and are easy to grow in your own garden and are available in supermarkets.

Dried herbs are also very good to use; here are some ideas on their uses: -

|  |  |
|---|---|
| Lemon balm | Summer drinks, jam and salad dressings. |
| Bay | Marinades, savoury dishes, rich stock and rice. |
| Borage | Candied flowers, punches and salads. |
| Tansy | Meats, eggs, salads, pancakes and cakes. |
| Chives | Salads, soups, cottage cheese and eggs. |
| Basil | Tomatoes, egg and meat dishes. |
| Comfrey | Alternative to spinach, use like celery. |
| Chervil | Add to soups, spinach and all egg dishes. |
| Dill | Fish dishes, yoghurt and sauces. |
| Thyme | Roast meat, poultry and bouquet garni. |
| Fennel | Fish dishes, meats and dressings for salads. |
| Rosemary | All meat, casseroles, fish, rice and egg dishes. |
| Mint | Sauces, jellies, summer drinks and mixed herbs. |
| Parsley | Casseroles, soups, salads, bouquet garni and fish dishes. |
| Marjoram | Stuffing, egg dishes, cheese dishes, meat & casseroles. |
| Tarragon | Meat dishes, salads, egg and cheese dishes. |
| Sage | Rich meats, chicken stuffing, salads, game sausages and cheeses. |
| Garlic | Fish, meat, vegetables, salads, flans, sauces & pasta dishes. |
| Savoury | Pork, meat, game and bean and lentil soups. |
| Salad Burnet | Salads, fruit cups, punches and summer wine. |

*(this list is from the previous editions of "Healthy Lifestyle Recipes". Please see the main chapter on herbs and spices on page 25, which is re-printed by kind permission of Schwartz Herbs and Spices.)*

## Five a Day

You may have attended one of the local road-shows that tour the country and have heard that the World Health Organisation now recommends that we eat 1lb of fresh fruit and vegetables every day, excluding potatoes. That is about five portions of fruit and vegetables a day to stay healthy. The reason is they are rich in anti-oxidant vitamins and minerals which help combat heart disease and cancer.

Vegetables are best cooked in a small amount of water or in a steamer. Micro-waving is also an excellent way of cooking vegetables since little water is needed, about three tablespoons on average or, in the case of frozen vegetables, usually none at all. Vegetables are also delicious eaten raw.

The following chart shows the various vitamin contents in certain foods: -

## Vitamin Table

| **Vitamin** | **What it is found in** |
| --- | --- |
| Vitamin A (Carotene) | Carrots, spinach, peppers, cheese, dried apricots, watercress & margarine. |
| Vitamin B1 (Thiamin) | Rice, bran, oatmeal, peas, whole-wheat bread and sunflower seeds. |
| Vitamin B2 (Riboflavin) | Mushrooms, prunes, broad-beans and almonds. |
| Vitamin B3 (Niacin) | Dried peaches, dates and sesame seeds. |
| Vitamin B6 (Pyridoxine) | Currants, bananas, bran and peanuts. |
| Vitamin B12 | Sosmix, yoghurt, milk, eggs and cheese. (Sosmix is a vegetable sausage mixture.) |
| Folic Acid | Spinach, broccoli, bran and nuts. |
| Biotin | Vegetables, pulses and yeast extract. |
| Pantothenic Acid | Found in all natural foods. |
| Vitamin C | Oranges, grapefruit, blackcurrant, parsley, broccoli, cabbages and strawberries. |
| Vitamin D | Sunlight enables the body to make vitamin D in the skin. Found in cheese, eggs, butter and fish, particularly oily fish. |
| Vitamin E | Vegetable oils, wheat-germ and nuts. |

*Many people have said they have benefited from attending HeartCare's Healthy Lifestyle events as this has enabled them to find out that their cholesterol levels etc., were higher than they should be. They have then visited their doctor who has taken steps to put this right*

*One of HeartCare's aims is to educate and encourage all, particularly the young, to lead a healthy lifestyle and reduce the possibility of heart disease.*

## *Conversion Charts*

These conversions are approximate. Always use the same measurements, either metric or imperial - **never** mix the two in one recipe

| Weights | |
|---|---|
| Metric | Imperial |
| 15g | ½ oz |
| 30g | 1 oz |
| 45g | 1½ oz |
| 60g | 2 oz |
| 75g | 2½ oz |
| 100g | 4 oz |
| 150g | 5 oz |
| 175g | 6 oz |
| 200g | 7 oz |
| 225g | 8 oz |
| 250g | 9 oz |
| 275g | 10 oz |
| 300g | 11 oz |
| 350g | 12 oz |
| 375g | 13 oz |
| 400g | 14 oz |
| 425g | 15 oz |
| 450g | 1 lb |
| 550g | 1¼ lb |
| 675g | 1½ lb |
| 800g | 1¾ lb |
| 900g | 2 lb |
| 1 kg | 2¼ lb |
| 1.5 kg | 3¼ lb |
| 2 kg | 4½ lb |

| Liquid | |
|---|---|
| Metric | Imperial |
| 15ml | ½ fl oz |
| 30ml | 1 fl oz |
| 60ml | 2 fl oz |
| 150ml | 5 fl oz/¼ pint |
| 275ml | 10 fl oz/½ pint |
| 570 ml | 20 fl oz/1 pint |
| 900 ml | 1½ pint |
| 1 litre | 1¾ pint |

| Oven Temperatures | | |
|---|---|---|
| °C | °F | Gas Mk |
| 140 | 275 | 1 |
| 150 | 300 | 2 |
| 170 | 325 | 3 |
| 180 | 350 | 4 |
| 190 | 375 | 5 |
| 200 | 400 | 6 |
| 220 | 425 | 7 |
| 230 | 450 | 8 |
| 240 | 475 | 9 |

# Starters

HeartCare Healthy Lifestyle Recipes - fourth edition - 2003

# *Healthy Lifestyle Pasta*
Serves 4

**Ingredients: -**
200g/8oz - coloured pasta twists, cooked and allowed to cool
100g/4oz - cooked peeled prawns, cold
6 - slices spring onions
¼ tsp - tomato sauce
1 x 325g - can sweet-corn - unsweetened and no added salt.
1 x 150ml - healthy eating natural bio yoghurt

**Method: -**
Combine all ingredients and mix well.

# Low Fat Vegetarian Pâté
(Serves 4)

**Ingredients: -**
1-large aubergine
100g/4oz - button mushrooms (chopped)
15ml/1 tbsp - dried coriander
10ml/2 tsp - lemon juice
2 - tomatoes, skinned, seeded and chopped
50ml/4 tbsp - wholemeal breadcrumbs
15ml/1 tbsp - olive oil
2 - cloves garlic, crushed
1.25m/¼ tsp - ground nutmeg
Pepper to taste

**Method: -**
Pierce the aubergine with a fork and place under a preheated grill.
Cook until the skin starts to split and the flesh is soft.
Turn 3 or 4 times to cook on all sides.
Place the olive oil, garlic and mushrooms in a saucepan and cook for 3 minutes.
Drain off any excess liquid.
Add the nutmeg, pepper, lemon juice, coriander and blend together.
Scoop out the flesh from the aubergine and place in a sieve and press lightly with a spoon to remove excess liquid.
Blitz the aubergine, tomato and the mushroom mixture until smooth.
Mix in the breadcrumbs - place in a bowl and cover and chill for 1-2 hours.
Serve with wholemeal toast and salad.

Always chose vegetables which look fresh. In general, fruit and vegetables have a higher vitamin content if their colour is dark.
Never add bi-carbonate of soda to vegetables as this destroys vitamin C.
Most meat pâtés are high in fat content but this vegetable pâté is a good alternative to meat and also provides a good supply of fibre.
Extra Virgin olive oil is the best to use, as this is the first pressing of the olives.
This recipe takes about 10 minutes to prepare and about 12 minutes to cook.

## Smoked Mackerel Pâté
(Serves 2 with salad for a good lunch or 4 as a starter)

**Ingredients: -**
2 - smoked mackerel fillets, skinned  (high in essential omega 3 oils)
1 x 250g - tub of quark
Horseradish sauce (to taste)
Lemon juice (to taste)

**Method:**
Blitz all the ingredients until they form a smooth pâté.
If you do not have a food processor, this can easily be done in a bowl with a fork.
Serve with hot toast.
The fish is oily, so you won't need butter.

## Tuna Pâté

**Ingredients: -**
1 - tin of tuna  (high in essential omega 3 oils)
1 - small piece of smoked mackerel   (high in essential omega 3 oils)
5ml/1 tsp - horseradish - optional
A little lemon juice
A little tomato ketchup

**Method: -**
Drain tuna and place in a bowl.
Take the mackerel remove skin and bones (if any) and add to the tuna.
Add all the other ingredients and mix thoroughly together.
Serve with toasted triangles or a selection of savoury biscuits plus a small salad or garnish if required and decorate the top of the pâté with lemon wedges and sprigs of parsley.

**Please visit our web site -  www.heartcarecsg.co.uk**

HeartCare Healthy Lifestyle Recipes - fourth edition - 2003

# *Soups*

# Country Tomato Soup
*serves 6*

**Ingredients: -**
3 tbs - sunflower oil
2 - onions, finely chopped
2 - garlic cloves, crushed
1¼ kg/2½lb - tomatoes, peeled and quartered
1 - bay leaf
1 tsp - dried thyme
900 ml/1½ pints - chicken stock, skimmed of all fat
½ kg/1lb - dried white haricot beans, soaked, cooked and drained
1 tbs - fresh parsley, chopped
Salt and black pepper

**Method: -**
Heat the oil in a saucepan.
Add the onions and garlic and fry until the onions are soft but not brown.
Stir in the tomatoes, bay leaf, thyme. Add salt and pepper to taste.
Cook gently, stirring occasionally, for 20 minutes or until the mixture is very thick.
Add the stock, bring to the boil and stir well.
Cover and simmer for 15 minutes.
Add the beans and cook for 5 minutes longer.
Turn into a tureen or individual soup bowls and sprinkle with parsley.

## *Italian Bean Soup*
Serves 4-6  (Low fat, high fibre, vegetarian)

**Ingredients: -**

225g/8oz - dried white beans, e.g. haricot or butter beans. Tinned beans could be used.
600ml/1 pint - water
1 - clove garlic, crushed
1 - large carrot, sliced
4 - tomatoes, skinned and chopped
1 - large onion, chopped
1 - celery stick, sliced
1 - bay leaf
30ml/2 tbsp - chopped parsley
Finely grated rind and juice of half a lemon
Salt and pepper

**Method: -**

Put the beans in a large bowl, cover with the water, leave to soak overnight, alternatively pour over some boiling water and soak for several hours.
Make up to 1·2litre/2 pints with stock or more water.
Place the beans and liquid in a large pan, add all the remaining ingredients except the parsley.
Bring to the boil and boil for 10 minutes to destroy the toxins in the beans, simmer for 1-1½ hours until the beans are tender, adding more water if necessary.
Discard the bay leaf.
Transfer half of the beans and liquid into an electric blender.
Return the puree to the soup and bring to the boil, stirring constantly.
Taste and adjust the seasoning.
Add more liquid if soup is too thick.
Sprinkle with parsley.

# Lentil and Lemon Soup
Serves 6 - Cooking time: 40 minutes

**Ingredients: -**
30m/2 tbsp - virgin olive oil
1 - large onion, chopped
1 - garlic clove - crushed
150g/5oz - red lentils, washed
600ml/1 pint - vegetable stock
1x400g/14oz tin - chopped tomatoes
30ml/2 tbsp - tomato puree
30ml/2 tbsp - finely chopped fresh thyme
salt & freshly ground pepper
juice of ½ lemon

**Garnish: -**
6 - small sprigs fresh thyme

**Method:-**
Heat the oil, cook onion and garlic gently for 10 minutes without colouring.
Add the lentils and stir to coat well in the oil.
Add the stock and bring to the boil - take off scum.
Add the tinned tomatoes, tomato puree and ¾ of the thyme.
Bring back to the boil and simmer, covered for 15-20 minutes stirring occasionally.
Taste for seasoning and add the remaining chopped fresh thyme.
Add the lemon juice little by little to taste.
Serve garnished with sprigs of thyme.

# Lettuce Soup
Serves 4

**Ingredients: -**
1 - lettuce or 6 - 8 outside leaves
1 - large onion
900ml/1½ pint - chicken stock
200ml/½ pint - cold water
2 - large dessert spoons skimmed milk powder
1 - large potato
Seasoning

**Method: -**
Wash and shred lettuce.
Roughly chop the onion and potato.
Place in a pan with the stock and simmer, uncovered, for 20/30 minutes.
Liquidise or sieve, add cold water, milk powder, seasoning and return to the boil, stirring.
This is delicious served hot or cold. You could also make this soup using sorrel in place of the lettuce.

# *Minestrone Soup*
Serves 6

**Ingredients: -**
1 - carrot, finely diced
30ml/2 tbsp - olive oil
1½ litre/2¾ pints - chicken or vegetable stock
2 - leeks thinly sliced
1 - clove garlic, crushed
100g/4oz - macaroni
50g/2oz - savoy cabbage, shredded
400g/14oz - tin tomatoes with onions
400g/14oz - tin cannelloni beans, drained
30ml/2 tbsp - chopped fresh basil
1 - onion finely diced
1 - bay leaf
100g/4oz - cauliflower
1 - courgette, sliced

**Method: -**
Fry the garlic, carrot, onion and cabbage in the oil, add the stock and bay leaf and bring to the boil.
Simmer for 3 minutes.
Add the leeks, cauliflower and pasta, and cook for 10 minutes.
Stir in the courgette, tomatoes and beans.
Simmer for 5 minutes and then add the basil.

*All beans, cannelloni, soya beans and lentils contain B group vitamins.*

# Tomato and Basil Soup

**Ingredients: -**
Approx 2 fl oz - extra virgin olive oil
1 - clove garlic, crushed
900g/2lb - large beefsteak tomatoes
900ml/1½ pint - chicken stock
2 - onions, chopped
45ml/3 tbsp - flour
30ml/2 tbsp - tomato puree
45ml/3 tbsp - fresh chopped basil
Pinch salt
Pinch freshly ground black pepper

**Method: -**
Cook onions and garlic for 2 or 3 minutes.
Halve the tomatoes and discard the seeds.
Remove the onion from the heat and stir in the flour, cook gently for 1 minute, stirring.
Gradually add the stock. Bring to the boil slowly continuing to cook until thickened.
Stir in the tomato puree, basil and tomatoes.
Season.
Cover the pan and simmer gently for 30 minutes.
Leave to cool a little, pour into a food processor or blender.
Process until smooth.

*Margarines which are called "hydrogenated" contain damaging fats called "trans fats".*

# Salads

## Bean and Pepper Salad
Serves 4

Mix together a large can of drained haricot or flageolet beans, rings of onion and green pepper, and skinned diced tomatoes.
Toss in a light vinaigrette dressing and arrange on a bed of lettuce.

## Bean Sprout Salad

**Ingredients: -**
450g/1lb - fresh or canned and drained bean sprouts
50g/2oz - canned pimento, drained and chopped
1 - pickled cucumber, chopped
1 tbsp - fresh chives, chopped
2 tbsp - sunflower oil
1 tbsp - wine vinegar
½ tsp - prepared mustard
2 tsp - soy sauce
½ tsp - sugar
Salt and pepper

**Method: -**
Put the bean sprouts, pimento, cucumber and chives in a salad bowl and toss well together.
Mix together the remaining ingredients with salt and pepper to taste and pour this dressing over the salad.
Toss well and chill for one hour before serving.

HeartCare Healthy Lifestyle Recipes - fourth edition - 2003

# Brown Rice, Lentil and Mushroom Salad

**Ingredients: -**
Brown rice - measured to 230ml/8fl oz level in jug
Boiling water - measured in same jug, to 460ml/16fl oz
225g/8 oz - whole brown lentils
15g/½ oz - extra virgin olive oil
100g/4 oz - mushrooms, wiped and thinly sliced
8 - spring onions, thinly sliced
½ - green pepper, chopped
15ml/1 tbs - finely chopped walnuts   (high in essential omega 3 oils)
1 x 150cm/6" - piece unpeeled cucumber, chopped
Salt

**Method: -**
Cook lentils in plenty of unsalted boiling water for 30 - 40 minutes until just soft.
In another pan melt butter, stir in rice to coat and pour in measured boiling water.
Stir once, cover and simmer for 40 - 45 minutes until rice is tender and has absorbed the liquid.
Combine drained lentils and rice while hot and dress with dressing.

**for the Dressing: -**
**Ingredients: -**
5 dsp - oil
50ml/1 dsp - wine vinegar
5ml/1 tsp - mustard powder
1 - clove garlic, crushed
Salt and black pepper
Shake well together

*NB. If not used to brown rice try brown basmati as it is a nice introduction.*

**Please visit our web site -  www.heartcarecsg.co.uk**

## *Korean Vegetable Salad* (serves 4-6)

**Ingredients: -**
1 - small turnip, peeled and cut into long thin strips
2 - 4 tbsp - sunflower oil
1 - small onion, finely chopped
125g/4oz - mushrooms, thinly sliced
2 - celery stalks, thinly sliced
3 - spring onions, chopped
1 - carrot, scraped and cut into long, thin strips
1 tbsp - pine nuts, finely chopped
salt

**Dressing: -**
3 tbsp - soy sauce
1 tbsp - brown sugar
1 tbsp - vinegar
½ tsp - ground ginger
black pepper

**Method: -**
Sprinkle the turnip strips with salt and set aside for 15 minutes.
Heat 2 tablespoons of the oil in a frying-pan.
Add the turnip strips and fry for 3 to 4 minutes or until they are crisp.
Transfer the turnip strips to kitchen paper towels to drain and cool.
Add the onion to the pan and fry until it is golden brown.
Add the onion to the turnip strips and leave to drain and cool.
Add the mushrooms to the pan, with more oil if necessary, and fry for 4 minutes, stirring frequently.
Transfer to kitchen paper towels to drain and cool.
Add the celery to the pan and fry until it is light gold.
Transfer to kitchen paper towels to drain and cool.
When the fried vegetables are cold, combine them with the spring onions and carrot in a serving dish.
Sprinkle over the pine nuts.
Mix together the dressing ingredients and pour over the salad.
Toss well and serve.

## *Low Calorie/Low fat dressing for Salad*

**Ingredients: -**
15ml/1 tbsp - lemon juice
15ml/1 tbsp - vinegar
15ml/1 tsp - chopped parsley
Salt, pepper and mustard to taste

**Method: -**
Mix together and use on your salads.

## Orange Salad
Serves 4 - 6

**Ingredients: -**
4 - Oranges
225g/8oz - bean sprouts
30ml/2 tbsp - well seasoned French dressing
15ml/1 tbsp - chopped parsley
1 x 425g/15oz can - red kidney beans
4 sticks - celery, sliced

**Method: -**
Using a sharp knife, remove the peel and pith from the oranges and cut into segments, free of any membrane, retain any juice.
Drain the beans well and place in a bowl with the orange segments, the retained juice and the bean sprouts and celery.
Add the dressing and parsley and toss well.

## Red Cabbage Coleslaw
(Low fat, high fibre)

**Ingredients: -**
100g/4oz - red cabbage, finely shredded
50g/2oz - white cabbage, finely shredded
4 sliced - spring onions
2 - grated carrots
25g/1oz - pine nuts or sunflower seeds (rich in healthy omega 6 oils)
50g/2oz - raisins
176ml/6 fl oz - low fat live yoghurt
15ml/1 tbsp - low fat mayonnaise
Freshly ground black pepper

**Method: -**
Mix shredded vegetables together and all other ingredients and toss to coat.

## Vinaigrette (French dressing)

**Ingredients: -**
150ml/¼ pint - virgin olive oil
1 - clove garlic, crushed
1¼ml/¼ tsp - mustard powder
1¼ml/¼ tsp - chopped fresh herbs of your choice or dried herbs
75ml/5 tbsp - wine vinegar
Pinch of sugar
Ground pepper
Pinch of salt

**Method: -**
Mix well together.

# Wild Rice and Asparagus Salad

Serves 4 - Preparation: 20 minutes - Cooking Time: 30 minutes

### Ingredients: -
225g/8oz - easy cook long grain wild rice
15ml/1 tbsp - olive oil
5ml/1 tsp - cayenne pepper
5ml/1 tsp - ground cumin
100g/4oz - asparagus tips
225g/8oz - baby sweet corn
¼ - melon, cut into cubes
50g/1¾oz - dried fruit
50g/1¾oz - whole blanched almonds

### for the Dressing: -
1 - garlic clove, finely chopped (optional)
30ml/2 tbsp - chopped, fresh parsley
30ml/2 tbsp - chopped, fresh coriander
30ml/2 tbsp - fresh lemon juice
60ml/4 tbsp - olive oil
Pepper

### Method: -
Place the rice in a large pan with 600ml/1 pint water, bring to the boil, then reduce the heat. Cover and simmer for 15-20 minutes until all the water has been absorbed and the rice is tender.
Heat the oil in a small frying pan, add half the spices and almonds.
Cook for 5-7 minutes until cooked, tossing regularly.
Bring a medium pan of water to the boil and blanch the sweet corn and asparagus for 3-4 minutes until tender.
Drain and refresh under cold water.
Place the rice in a large serving bowl and mix in the lemon and dried fruit.
Mix together all the ingredients for the dressing, pour half over the rice, mix and season.
Arrange the rice with the asparagus and sweet corn on serving plates.
Drizzle with the remaining dressing and sprinkle with the remaining spices and almonds.

HeartCare Healthy Lifestyle Recipes - fourth edition - 2003

# *Herbs and Spices*

*The information and pictures in this chapter have been re-produced with the kind permission of Schwartz Herbs and Spices.*

www.schwartz.co.uk

Cathy Richards on 01844 292930.

cathy.richards@mccormick.co.uk

# Herbs

**Basil** *(Ocimum basilicum)*     Use 1-2 tsp for 4 servings

## Description
Basil is a herb with spicy overtones of aniseed and is strongly associated with Italian cooking.
Basil complements - tomatoes, green vegetables, salads, soups, eggs, fish, cheese, lamb, pizza and pasta sauces.
Basil is delicious with tomatoes, cooked or as a salad.

## Did you know?
Basil has a strong history of reverence and loathing. Its name is Greek for "King" and it is revered as a sacred herb in the Hindu religion. However, in Europe during the Middle Ages it was believed that scorpions would breed under pots of Basil and just to smell Basil would form a scorpion in the brain.
Basil is known as the tomato herb because of their affinity. There are over 150 varieties of Basil.

## Quality
Basil should have a good fresh green colour preserved by careful drying at temperatures of less than 110°F. The dried herb should retain its aniseed flavour. Methyl Chavicol is the principal flavour - giving volatile oil.

## Usage
For salads make a dressing of olive oil and lemon juice with Schwartz Minced Garlic and a sprinkling of Basil, salt and pepper.
Bake whole baby courgettes in olive oil, chopped tomato and Basil.
Add a teaspoon or two of Basil to tomato sauce and soups such as gazpacho.
Sprinkle Basil onto pizzas and pasta, together with Oregano, for an authentic Italian flavour.
Sprinkle a mixture of Basil, salt, Cumin and Coriander onto lamb chops before grilling.

## Bay Leaves *(Laurus nobilis)*   Use 2-3 Bay Leaves for 4 servings

### Description
Bay Leaves have an astringent, spicy flavour similar to freshly ground pepper but without the heat. Dried Bay Leaves have a more intense and less bitter flavour than fresh.
To release the volatile oils encapsulated in the dried leaf, tear or break the leaves before adding to your cooking. Remove before serving. For decoration leave whole.

### Did You Know?
The bay tree grows wild and the leaves are harvested by cutting the branches and drying them in the shade. In ancient Greece and Rome the branches were used as wreaths to crown the victors in battle, sport and the arts. We still use the term poet laureate. The word baccalaureate means laurel berries and signifies the successful completion of one's studies.

### Quality
Good quality Bay Leaves should be large and whole with clean unblemished leaves of a good green colour. Eugenol is the principal flavour - giving volatile oil.

### Usage
Bay Leaves complement casseroles, stews, soups, sauces, stock, gravy, minced beef and milk puddings.
Add extra flavour to stews, casseroles and gravy by simmering with a torn Bay Leaf.
Bay Leaves add extra flavour to Italian Bolognese sauce and other minced meat dishes.
The strength and flavour of Bay increases with cooking time.

### Chives *(Allium schoenoprasum)*     Use 2-3 tsp for 4 servings

**Description**
Chives have a mild, fresh, onion flavour and bright green colour.
Chives complement - eggs, cheese, potatoes, salads, soups, fish and chicken and are excellent as a garnish.

**Did You Know?**
Chives grow in the cooler Northern hemisphere. Dutch farmers have even been known to use them as fodder for their cows to produce chive-flavoured milk. Chives are cut in July before they flower and are processed quickly to avoid deterioration of their delicate flavour. Chives, together with Parsley, Tarragon and Chervil make up the classic French "Fine Herbes".

**Quality**
The delicate flavour of Chives is preserved by quick freeze-drying immediately following cutting and processing. Their colour should be bright green.

**Usage**
Add Chives to cooked dishes at the last minute to preserve their delicate flavour.
The distinctive flavour of Chives adds interest to bland dishes. Sprinkle onto omelettes, cottage cheese and potatoes.
Add a bright finish to all types of salads, such as green, potato and pasta, with a sprinkling of chives

## Coriander Leaf *(Coriandum sativum)*      Use 1-2 tsp for 4 servings

### Description
The flavour of Coriander Leaf is strong, pungent and earthy. It is quite different from the aromatic, citrus flavour of Coriander Seed.
Although both are from the same plant they are not interchangeable.
Coriander Leaf is used extensively in Asian, Oriental and Latin American cooking.
Coriander Leaf complements - chicken, fish, curries, rice, tomatoes, Thai, Indonesian, Chinese and South American dishes.

### Did You Know?
Coriander Leaf is the world's most popular herb. Whilst it is not often found in European cooking, it is used extensively in Asian, Oriental, Middle Eastern and Latin American dishes.

### Quality
Coriander Leaves should have a good green colour. The flavour and aroma of the dried leaves become more apparent once added to the cooked dish.

### Usage
Mexican salsas make delicious dips and hot or cold sauces. They are excellent as "chutneys" with a cold buffet or used with traditional Mexican dishes.
Simply combine chopped tomatoes, onion, Garlic and Crushed Chillies with a tablespoon of Coriander Leaf.
For an Indian raita, stir chopped or grated cucumber, Coriander Leaf, salt and pepper into natural yoghurt.
A Thai style fresh chutney makes an excellent accompaniment to fish. Warm creamed coconut with lemon juice and stir in Coriander Leaf, Crushed Chillies and chopped spring onions.
Stir Coriander Leaf, Parsley, fresh green chillies, Garlic and onion into cooked rice to make Mexican arroz verde.
Add Coriander Leaf to breads, stuffing and sauces and sprinkle over spicy or creamy dishes at the end of cooking.

## Dill *(Anethum graveolens)*   Use 2-3 tsp for 4 servings
### Description
Dill has a fresh, sweet, anise-like flavour and aroma.
Dill complements - chicken, fish, minced meat, vegetables, eggs, cheese, salads, soups, pickles and is used as a garnish.
Dill is used to flavour baby cucumbers in Dill pickles.
Dill is an excellent seasoning for seafood, fish and new potatoes. It has a special affinity with salmon, both fresh and cured, as in gravadlax.

### Did You Know?
The word "Dill" comes from an old Norse word meaning 'to lull' due to their belief in the herb's soothing and sedative effect, especially for crying babies suffering from colic. The Greeks used Dill as a remedy for hiccups. In the Middle Ages Dill was used in many magic potions, including a protection against witchcraft.

### Quality
Dill should have a fresh green colour and mild flavour. D-Carvone is the principal flavour - giving volatile oil.

### Usage
For a coleslaw style dish, mix together minced onion, diced celery and shredded cabbage and toss in a dressing of soured cream, lemon juice and Dill.
Sprinkle Dill onto vegetables such as carrots, corn, green beans and peas.
Add Dill to Greek egg and lemon sauce for chicken, stuffed cabbage or vine leaves. In Greece, Dill is used to flavour minced beef dishes, much like parsley.
Use Dill as a refreshing alternative to parsley in omelettes, quiches and salads.
Mix into cream cheese.

## Marjoram & Oregano *(Marjorana hortensis & Origanum vulgare)*
Use 1-2 tsp for 4 servings

### Description
Marjoram is a sweet-scented herb characteristic of the Mediterranean. Marjoram complements - lamb, chicken, veal, pork, fish, pizza, tomatoes, vegetables, cheese, eggs, stuffing, Italian and Mexican dishes.

### Did You Know?
In Greek 'Oregano' means 'Joy of the mountains' from where it is gathered. It is used extensively in Greece and its many varieties are known as 'rigani'. Marjoram is a traditional herb in Bouquet Garni.

### Quality
Both Marjoram and Oregano should have a good colour, even sized leaf pieces and fresh aromatic aroma and flavour. Carvacrol is the principal flavour-giving volatile oil.

### Usage
Marinate and baste lamb or chicken with a dressing of olive oil, lemon juice, salt and Marjoram. Grill or barbecue and serve with wedges of lemon.
A similar dressing, perhaps with the addition of Crushed Chillies, can be used with fresh sardines.
Marjoram, as a sweet herb, gives milk puddings a special flavour.
Sprinkle Marjoram onto a green salad.

## Mint *(Mentha spicata)*   Use 1-2 tsp for 4 servings

### Description
Mint has a strong refreshing flavour, which adds an extra dimension to both sweet and savoury dishes.
Mint complements - lamb, veal, rabbit, new potatoes, peas, vegetables, salads, tomatoes, soups, jelly, fresh fruits.
Whilst traditionally used in the UK as a summer herb for flavouring lamb, new potatoes and peas, Mint is used in many dishes from the Middle East. It is one of the ingredients in Tunisian hot chilli sauce, often used as a table sauce, or as an ingredient in meat and vegetable stews.

### Did You Know?
The Latin name 'mentha' comes from 'menthe', a charming nymph who was changed into the Mint plant by Proserpine, the wife of Pluto, in a fit of jealousy. Mint symbolises hospitality. It repels rats and mice, relieves wasp stings and was used by the Romans to whiten teeth.

### Quality
Dried Mint should have a good green colour and a strong Mint flavour. If kept well sealed and away from sunlight it will not lose these properties.

### Usage
Tabbouleh is a Middle Eastern speciality made with Bulgar wheat, tomatoes, Mint, Parsley and lemon juice.
In India, Mint is used in raitas as a refreshing side dish to hot curries.
Mint tea is especially refreshing in summer and is excellent as a digestive.
Sprinkle Mint onto green salads.
In Greece, dolmades is a dish of cabbage or vine leaves stuffed with a mixture of rice, minced lamb, tomatoes, onions, Parsley and Mint, simmered in a little water and served with an egg and lemon sauce.
Aubergine with yoghurt sauce, bonjam borani is a dish, which combines three ingredients essential to Afghanistan cooking: Garlic, Mint and yoghurt.

### Parsley *(Petroselinum crispum)*     Use 1-2 tsp for 4 servings

**Description**
Parsley is probably the most popular and versatile herb available. It has a very mild, fresh flavour.
Parsley complements - lamb, chicken, ham, casseroles, fish, vegetables, salads, egg and cheese dishes, soups, sauces.

**Did You Know?**
The Greeks used Parsley to crown victors at the Isthmian Games. It was also a symbol of death and scattered over tombs. The Romans were the first to use Parsley as food and ate it like lettuce. The Romans believed Parsley worn as wreaths around their necks prevented drunkenness. Parsley has always been linked to the occult. It was believed that the seed germinated slowly because it had to go down to the devil and back seven times before it would grow. An old saying goes 'Where Parsley thrives, the missus is master'.

**Quality**
Parsley should have a good fresh green colour, even leaf particles and a mild aroma.

**Usage**
Parsley is an essential part of Bouquet Garni.
Gremolata is a garnish of grated lemon rind, Garlic and Parsley sprinkled over the traditional Italian dish, osso bucco. Sauté mushrooms in butter, Garlic and a good tablespoon of Parsley. Add Parsley to white sauce and creamy dips to give colour and a mild flavour.
Toss a tablespoon of Parsley into all salads, e.g. potato, pasta, lentil and green salads.
Parsley is a good garnish for white fish, as it will not overpower the delicate flavour.
Whilst French cuisine does not use a wide variety of herbs and spices, Parsley is used to flavour many dishes such as the well-known jambon persillé. This dish, made with chopped ham in aspic, flavoured with Parsley, Garlic and vinegar is excellent for buffets.

HeartCare Healthy Lifestyle Recipes - fourth edition - 2003

## Rosemary *(Rosmarinus officinalis)*     Use 1-2 tsp for 4 servings

### Description
Rosemary is the hard, needle-shaped leaf of a small evergreen shrub. It has a distinctive pinewood aroma and a strong bittersweet flavour.
Rosemary complements - lamb, pork, chicken, oily fish, game, tomato sauce, vegetables, soups, marinades

### Did You Know?
The Latin name 'Ros Maris' means 'Dew of the Sea', as the plant grows well by the seaside. Legend has it that the Virgin Mary, fleeing from Herod's soldiers, hung her cloak on a Rosemary bush one night. In the morning the white flowers had turned blue under her cloak. From then on, the herb became known as 'Rose of Mary'. In ancient Greece it was believed that Rosemary fortified the brain and refreshed the memory. Students wore it in their hair during examinations to improve their memory. Associated with remembrance, Rosemary was used at weddings and funerals. Rosemary is believed to grow well in the garden of a happy household. For a refreshing bath add a handful of Rosemary, tied in muslin, to the water. An infusion of Rosemary is said to be calming on the nerves. Rosemary is an antiseptic and works well as a breath freshener.

### Quality
Rosemary retains its flavour best as whole 'needles' but as these can be difficult to chew, Schwartz Rosemary is chopped for convenience into smaller particles. Cineole is the principal flavour - giving volatile oil.

### Usage
Rosemary is traditionally used with lamb but also goes well with pork. Its fresh, camphor-like aroma is a good counter-balance to rich or fatty foods. Gently simmer a boned and rolled loin of pork in milk flavoured with olive oil, butter, Garlic and a tablespoon of Rosemary.
Serve sliced in its own sauce, well reduced.
Rosemary adds flavour to fruit salads and jellies.
Sprinkle Rosemary over barbecue coals for an aromatic smoky flavour.
Rosemary makes a fresh and flavoursome marinade for meats and oily fish together with olive oil, Garlic and lemon juice. For duck and other game, serve a rich red wine and orange gravy flavoured with Rosemary.

HeartCare Healthy Lifestyle Recipes - fourth edition - 2003

**Sage**  *(Salvia officinalis)*     Use 1-2 tsp for 4 servings

### Description
Sage is the pale green leaf of an evergreen shrub. Its strong, fresh flavour makes it a popular culinary herb, but it has always been well known for its medicinal properties.
Sage complements - pork, veal, game, poultry, sausages, vegetables, salads, onion, cheese, eggs, stuffing, coatings.

### Did You Know?
It was believed that Sage strengthened the memory; hence a sage or wise man would have a long memory. Sage tea is believed to make a good tonic and blood cleanser. Used as a mouthwash Sage is said to freshen the breath and help in alleviating bleeding gums. A Sage bath helps ease rheumatism and aching limbs.

### Quality
Sage should be silvery-grey and strongly aromatic. It has a medicinal pinewood flavour. Thujone is the principal flavour-giving volatile oil.

### Usage
Sage has an affinity with fatty foods, especially pork and cheese. Sausages and faggots are often flavoured with Sage.
It is used in traditional sage and onion stuffing. Saltimbocca is an Italian dish meaning 'jump in the mouth'! Thin slices of veal are seasoned with a sprinkling of Sage, overlaid with a slice of prosciutto, then quickly fried and served with Mozzarella melted over. Sprinkle a little Sage into salads for a refreshing flavour.
Combine a little Sage with cheese and breadcrumbs for topping grilled fish. Season the simmering beans and vegetables of minestrone soup with Sage for extra flavour.
Add Sage to the breadcrumb coating of Scotch eggs.

SAGE

## Tarragon  *(Artemesia dracunculus)*   Use 1-2 tsp for 4 serving

### Description
The long narrow leaves of Tarragon have a strong, spicy, anise flavour.
Tarragon complements - chicken, fish, veal, lamb, eggs, salads, sauces, vegetables, vinegar, soups, mayonnaise.
Use Tarragon sparingly as it can overpower other ingredients and take on a bitter taste.

### Did You Know?
The name Tarragon is probably a corruption of the French word 'estragon' meaning 'little dragon' as the roots curl around like a dragon's tail. Tarragon was used to cure the bites of dogs and poisonous snakes. Tarragon is one of the classic French herbs and is a favourite flavouring for white wine vinegar. Tarragon is a stimulant to the appetite.

### Quality
The quality of Tarragon is determined by its good green colour, a strong anise flavour and volatile oil content. Methyl chavicol is the principal flavour-giving volatile oil.

### Usage
Tarragon has an affinity with chicken, as in the classic dish poulet à l estragon. Flavour classic sauce béarnaise with Tarragon.
Tarragon is superb in salads, with fish and with egg dishes such as omelette and eggs baked in cream.
Rémoulade sauce made with mayonnaise, mustard, chopped pickle, capers and Tarragon is traditionally served with fish, meat, poultry and vegetables.
Glazed carrots or carrot salad can be given a distinctive flavour with a sprinkling of Tarragon.

**Please visit our web site -  www.heartcarecsg.co.uk**

### Thyme *(Thymus vulgaris)*     Use 1-2 tsp for 4 servings

**Description**
Thyme is a small, woody-stemmed plant with tiny grey-green leaves and pretty little purple flowers. It is at its most aromatic when grown in hot, sunny, dry conditions and a light sandy soil.
Thyme complements - chicken, lamb, beef, offal, rabbit, turkey, vegetables, fish, cheese, eggs, soups, stews, & casseroles.

**Did You Know?**
Records of Thyme date back to ancient Greece where it symbolised courage. Roman soldiers bathed in water infused with Thyme to gain vigour, courage and strength. Thyme has antiseptic qualities. It also aids the digestion of fatty food. Laid amongst clothes it is said to keep fleas and moths away.

**Quality**
Good quality Thyme should contain very little twig or stalk. Its aroma and flavour should be strong and fresh. Thymol is the principal flavour-giving volatile oil.

**Usage**
The strong fresh flavour of Thyme blends well with other herbs without overpowering them. It is one of the ingredients in Bouquet Garni.
Thymes aromatic flavour adds warmth and pungency to a very wide variety of dishes such as stuffing, marinades, vegetables, fish and cheese. It is an essential flavouring in many classic dishes for meat, game and poultry. Slow-cooked dishes, such as French daubes, cassoulets and navarins are all flavoured with Thyme.
Traditional British dishes are often flavoured with Thyme, especially those with fatty cuts of meat or rich game. Add Thyme to Irish stew, faggots, liver and onions, oxtail, boiled bacon, steak and kidney and Lancashire hotpot.

HeartCare Healthy Lifestyle Recipes - fourth edition - 2003

# *Spices*

**Allspice**  *(Pimenta dioica)*        Use 1/2-1 tsp for 4 servings

Description
Allspice is the dried, unripe berry of a tree indigenous to the Caribbean and Central America. As its name implies it tastes of a mixture of cinnamon, nutmeg and cloves.
Allspice complements - beef, pork, chicken, sausages, fish, cheese, pickles, stewed fruit, cakes, biscuits.

**Did you know?**
Columbus introduced Allspice to Europe in the 16th Century. It is one of the few spices native to the Western hemisphere and, although many attempts have been made to grow Allspice in other parts of the world, it remains the only spice commercially produced exclusively in this area. Allspice was originally used by American Indians to preserve meat and fish. The term buccaneer comes from the Allspice cured meats of the Arawak Indians, called boucan, adopted by the pirates using the island of Jamaica as a base for raiding shipping.

**Quality**
Allspice berries from Jamaica have the highest oil content and a dark reddish-brown colour. Eugenol is the principal flavour-giving volatile oil.

**Usage**
Ideal sprinkled on gammon and pork steaks, just mix with orange juice, a little honey or brown sugar and oil and brudh on before grilling.
Sprinkle into beef or lamb casseroles for an extra warming flavour.
Stir into fruit salad or stewed fruit for extra flavour.
Use in many Caribbean dishes for an authentic taste.

HeartCare Healthy Lifestyle Recipes - fourth edition - 2003

**Caraway Seed** *(Carum carvi)*   Use 1-2 tsp for 4 servings

### Description
Caraway Seed has a warm, pungent, slightly bitter flavour with aniseed overtones. Caraway complements - cabbage, potatoes, onion, carrots, coleslaw, sauerkraut, pork, goulash, dumplings, cheese, pickles, cakes, biscuits, rye bread,

### Did you know?
Caraway aids the digestion. Caraway was known in England from the 14th Century. It was popular in seed cake and breads as well as with cabbage and bean dishes. Caraway oil is used in liqueurs, perfume and mouthwashes.

### Quality
Caraway Seeds should have a uniform shape and consistent creamy brown colour with no stem or chaff content. Carvone is the principal flavour-giving volatile oil.

### Usage
Thinly slice white cabbage. Stir-fry in a little olive oil and butter and sprinkle in a tsp Caraway Seed. Serve once the cabbage is hot but still crisp.
For seed cake just stir 1 tbs Caraway Seed into a plain sponge cake mixture.
Cut peeled carrots into strips and cook for 5 minutes in a little water with 1 tbs lemon juice, 1 tsp sugar, 1 tsp Caraway Seed and a knob of butter. Boil to reduce the liquid and leave the carrots lightly glazed.

**Cardamom**  *(Elettaria cardamomum)*     Use 1-2 tsp for 4 servings

### Description
Cardamom pods contain highly aromatic citrus-like, floral flavoured seeds with menthol undertones.
Either crush the pod lightly and discard after cooking, or open and remove the seeds which can then be used whole or ground. The outer green pod is not eaten.
Cardamom complements - fish, meat, curries, rice, fruit, pastries, meringue, cream, yoghurt, pickles.

### Did you know?
Cardamom is known as the Queen of spices (pepper is the King). Cardamom is said to have a cooling effect on the body. Chewing Cardamom seeds disguises the smell of alcohol on the breath. Cardamom is renowned as a powerful aphrodisiac.

### Quality
India and Guatemala produce excellent quality Cardamom. The pale green pods should be plump, unblemished and filled with dark, often sticky black or brown seed. Cineole is the principal flavour-giving volatile oil.

### Usage
Cardamom is an ingredient in Garam Masala and adds its unique flavour to curries.
In India, a spiced tea is made by boiling milk and water with 2 Whole Green Cardamoms, a piece of Cinnamon, 3 Cloves and sugar to taste.
Cardamom adds spice to coffee in Arab countries and is popular in pastries and cakes in Scandinavia. It is a principal seasoning in Danish pastries.
Add flavour to a fresh fruit salad by simmering a teaspoon of lightly crushed Cardamoms in 125 ml (4 fl oz) of water and 2 tbs sugar for 5 minutes. Allow to cool and remove the pods. Add 125 ml (4 fl oz) orange juice and pour over a selection of sliced fresh fruits before chilling.
When cooking rice to accompany an Indian dish, add 6 Whole Green Cardamoms, 6 whole Cloves, 1/2 a Cinnamon Stick and 3 Bay Leaves for 4-6 servings. This gives a subtle spicy flavour.

# HeartCare Healthy Lifestyle Recipes - fourth edition - 2003

**Chillies** *(Capsicum frutescens)*     Use 1-2 whole chillies for 4 servings

### Description
Chillies are the pods of an annual plant of the Capsicum family. There are many different varieties whose subtleties of flavour are as varied as their heat levels which range from mild to fiery hot.
The majority of the heat in Chillies comes from the membranes. To reduce the heat remove before cooking.
Chillies are widely used in Indian, Mexican and South East Asian cookery.

### Did you know?
There are over 200 identified varieties of Chilli grown throughout the tropics. In addition there are many local varieties which have not yet been documented. Chillies contain capsaicin which gives them their fiery heat. Depending upon the variety, the heat scale measured in Scoville units, can range form
0-300,000. Chillies were introduced to Europe and India in the 15th and 16th centuries following their discovery in Central America. Explorers in the New World mistook the fiery heat of the Chilli (Capsicum) for pepper (Piper nigrum) and, therefore, named their discovery Pepper, to the confusion of future
generations. The sweet bell pepper, potatoes and tomatoes are all members of the same family as chilli peppers.

### Quality
Dried whole Chillies should be a deep rich red colour and fairly pliable.
Cayenne Pepper should have a bright red colour and fresh, pungent smell.
Schwartz Hot and Mild Chili Powders provide an especially harmonious blend of flavours brought about by the special Schwartz caramelisation process.

### Usage
The longer Chillies are cooked, the hotter the dish will become. Use whole chillies so that they can be easily removed at the end of cooking.
Flavour the oil for stir fries by frying 1-2 Whole Chillies for a few minutes, then remove before adding the other ingredients. Add whole in marinades before barbecuing or grilling.
Take care when handling Chillies - wear rubber gloves if possible. Avoid touching your eyes as the capsaicin will make them sting.
 Use to add heat to Mexican chili con carne, Indian and Thai curries and savoury mince.
Add Whole Chillies to pickles for extra bite and visual appeal.

### **Cinnamon** *(Cinnamomum)*   Use 1-2 sticks for 4 servings

## Description
Cinnamon is the peeled and curled inner bark of a tropical evergreen tree. It has a warm, sweet, woody aroma.
Cinnamon complements - beef, pork, curries, spinach, stewed fruits, sweet and savoury rice, cakes, biscuits, puddings, pickles, mulled wine, chocolate.

## Did you know?
The best Cinnamon grows within sight of the sea in a sub-tropical climate. Before the source of spices was discovered by Europeans, the Arabs maintained their monopoly of the spice trade by claiming that Cinnamon was harvested from the nests of ferocious birds and had to be gathered under their attack.

## Quality
Cinnamon Sticks should be an even, soft brown colour and quite slim. A pale coloured bark shows the finest quality. Whole Cinnamon Sticks have only a faint aroma but once broken or ground the volatile oils are released giving off their powerfully warm, sweet, pungent flavours. Cinnamic Aldehyde is the principal flavour-giving oil.

## Usage
Cinnamon is an important ingredient in Garam Masala, the Indian blend of warm spices used to add extra flavour to curries towards the end of cooking. Stir hot chocolate drinks with a Cinnamon Stick as they do in Mexico.
Cinnamon is an essential ingredient in Moroccan tagines or lamb stew.
Cinnamon, Coriander and Cloves are excellent in mulled wine.
Add a rich warm, spicy aroma to your Christmas tree with bundles of Cinnamon Sticks tied in bright red ribbon and decorated with a sprig of holly. Remember to remove the sticks before serving.

**Cloves** *(Syzygium aromaticum)*     Use according to taste

### Description
Cloves are the dried, unopened flower buds of a small evergreen tree.
They have a strong sweet, pungent flavour.
Cloves can have an overpowering flavour if used to excess and are often combined with other spices, as in Chinese Five Spice, Garam Masala and Mixed Spice, where they give warmth and body to dishes.

### Did you know?
The name Clove is derived from the French word *clou* meaning nail, which is the shape that the bud and stem resemble. In Indonesia half of the Clove production is mixed with tobacco to produce Kretek cigarettes. Cloves are known to have antisceptic properties and their smell is often associated with the dentist. Their use as a preservative in pickles and spiced dishes is well documented. At the time of the early Chinese civilisation commoners chewed Cloves to sweeten their breath before talking to the emperor. The chinese also used Cloves as a mild anaesthetic for toothache.

### Quality
Cloves should be large, plump and oily with a warm, reddish brown colour. The majority of the flower buds should be intact. Eugenol is the principal flavour-giving volatile oil.

### Usage
Cloves complement - ham, gammon, onions, rice, apples, cakes, biscuits, desserts, mulled wine, Chinese and Indonesian dishes.
Add Whole Cloves to mulled wine with Cinnamon Sticks and Coriander Seeds.
To combat the chills of winter, warm a tot of Irish whisky with 2 Whole Cloves, a dash of lemon juice and a pinch of sugar.
An onion studded with one or two Cloves gives steak & kidney pie, beef casseroles and bread sauce a warm, full flavour.
Stud baked or roasted ham with Whole Cloves and spread over a mixture of honey, sugar and mustard before finishing in a hot oven.

HeartCare Healthy Lifestyle Recipes - fourth edition - 2003

**Coriander Seed**  (Coriandum sativum)     Use 1-2 tsp for 4 servings

## Description
Coriander seed has a mild, sweet, slightly pungent, citrus-like flavour with a hint of sage.
Coriander complements - pork, curries, Middle Eastern dishes, vegetables, stewed fruit, chutney, pickles, cakes, biscuits, lentils.

## Did you know?
Both the seeds and leaves (see Coriander Leaf-Cilantro) are used in cooking but are not interchangeable as they have distinctly different flavours.
Coriander is known to have been used in Egypt since 1550BC for culinary and medicinal purposes. India is the largest producer of Coriander which is used extensively in curry powders.

## Quality
Coriander Seeds should be a uniform, light brown colour, an even size and unblemished. D-Linalool is the principal flavour - giving volatile oil.

## Usage
Lightly crush Coriander Seeds and fry in a little oil before adding baby spinach leaves. Toss until wilted and warmed through.
Crushed Coriander Seed and Bay Leaves add a mouth-watering flavour to mushrooms cooked à la Grècque. Sprinkle with olive oil and lemon juice before serving.
Afelia is cubed pork marinated and cooked in olive oil, red wine and crushed Coriander Seed.
Eastern recipes often contain Coriander Seed. Baharat, a seasoning blend from the Middle East, contains Nutmeg, Coriander, Cumin, Cloves, Cinnamon, Cardamoms, Paprika and Chilli and is used to spice meat and vegetables.

**Cumin Seed**  *(Cuminum cyminum)*     Use 1-2 tsp for 4 servings

### Description
Cumin has an earthy, pungent, aromatic flavour which is slightly bitter but not hot. Cumin complements - chicken, lamb, cheese, vegetables, rice, lentils, curries, Mexican dishes, tomato sauce, bread.

### Did you know?
Cumin was used by the Romans in place of Pepper. It was also ground to a paste and spread on bread. Cumin is said to keep lovers faithful and was often used in love potions. It has been used as a condiment in England since the 13th century and was a taxable import into London from 1419.

### Quality
Cumin Seed should be even sized and yellowish-brown with a strong, earthy aroma when ground. It should be carefully cleaned and sorted to remove extraneous matter. Cuminaldehyde is the principal flavour-giving volatile oil.

### Usage
Lightly dry roasting the seeds before use enhances their unique flavour and aroma.
Cumin has an affinity with dried beans and pulses. It is also an excellent spice for vegetables and is often used in conjunction with Coriander Seed.
Many traditional dishes are spiced with Cumin, or blends which include Cumin, such as ras-el-hanout from the Middle East and Garam Masala from India.
Cumin is an essential ingredient in curry powders and blends.

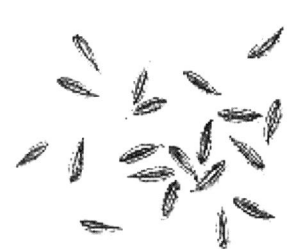

**Fennel Seed** *(Foeniculum vulgare)*     Use 1-2 tsp for 4 servings

### Description
Fennel Seeds are oval, light brown and have a subtle, sweet anise-like flavour. Fennel complements - fish, pork, veal, potatoes, rice, eggs, cheese, pickles, apples.

### Did you know?
Ancient Chinese and Hindus used Fennel as a remedy for snake bites and scorpion stings. In the Middle Ages it was hung over doorways to ward off evil spirits. Indians chew Fennel Seeds at the end of a meal to aid digestion and freshen the breath. Greek athletes ate Fennel to keep up their strength and keep down their weight.

### Quality
Good quality Fennel Seed should be clean with an anise-like flavour and aroma. The colour of the seeds ranges from yellow to greenish-brown. Anethole is the principal flavour - giving volatile oil.

### Usage
Fennel has a special affinity with fish. Try adding it to the basting juices during cooking.
Fennel counteracts the oiliness in fish and fattiness in meats such as pork.
In Italy, it is used to season salmon and a salami called finocchiona.
In India, Fennel Seeds are used in vegetarian dishes.
Make a savoury dressing for grilled monk fish with crushed Fennel Seeds, olive oil, red wine vinegar, chopped onion and salt.
Add extra flavour to potato salad and rice dishes with crushed Fennel Seeds.
Flavour risotto with Fennel Seeds and Parmesan cheese.
Serve baked fish seasoned with Fennel, lemon juice and dry white wine on a bed of pasta for a light summer supper.
Greek kakavia, a fish soup, uses Fennel to enhance the flavour of the fish, shellfish and tomatoes.

**Fenugreek**  *(Trigonella foenum-graecum)*     Use 1-2 tsp for 4 servings

### Description
Fenugreek has a strong, pungent aroma and a bitter 'curry-like' flavour which often dominates curry powders.
Fenugreek complements - curries, pickles, chutneys.

### Did you know?
Fenugreek was used as a conditioning powder to give horses a glossy coat, and was reputed to cure baldness in men. Harem women ate roasted Fenugreek to develop a buxom figure. The Egyptians used Fenugreek for incense and embalming. Made into a paste and spread over the body, Fenugreek is supposed to reduce fever. Fenugreek restores nitrogen in the soil as it comes from the pea family.

### Quality
Ground Fenugreek has a warm, yellowish-brown colour with a strong curry-like flavour.

### Usage
Fenugreek is used in a variety of spice mixes, such as sambhar powder, which flavours Southern Indian vegetable and dhal dishes, and Ethiopian berbere, a hot and spicy blend for seasoning stews.
Curry powders and Indian spice mixes for chutneys and pickles include ground Fenugreek.

HeartCare Healthy Lifestyle Recipes - fourth edition - 2003

**Garlic  (Allium sativum)**        Use 1/4 - 1/2 tsp for 4 servings

### Description
Garlic is one of the most widely used spices in the world. Dried garlic can usually be used in place of fresh and is more convenient.
These fine granules of pure garlic give savoury dishes a mouth-watering flavour without the texture of fresh chopped garlic.

### Did you know?
The workers building the Pyramids ate Garlic to keep up their strength and avoid illness. Nowadays, Garlic bread is the UK's most popular restaurant starter. At one time, Garlic was said to keep vampires away! Garlic is highly antiseptic - it purifies and thins the blood. Garlic is said to be an antidote to drunkeness. The chlorophyll in Parsley helps clear the breath of Garlic odours.

### Quality
Blends incorporating both garlic and onion readily absorb moisture. They should be kept away from steam and stored in well sealed containers. However, if they do become solid in the jar just stir to loosen the granules before using.

### Usage
Add to most savoury dishes, including sauces, marinades, casseroles, soups and stuffing.
Sprinkle into salads such as coleslaw, pasta and rice.
Add Garlic Granules to Yorkshire pudding batter.
Marinade olives in olive oil, Garlic Granules and Oregano.
Rub a leg of lamb with Garlic Granules, salt and Rosemary before roasting.

**Ginger** *(Zingiber officinale)*     Use 1-2 tsp for 4 servings

## Description
Ginger has a warm, sweet aroma and a hot, biting flavour.
Ginger complements - curries, stir-fries, ham, gammon, fish, fruit, biscuits, cakes, puddings, pickles, chutney, Oriental and South East Asian dishes.

## Did you know?
Ginger is a warming spice said to promote sweating and relieve colds. A teaspoon of Ginger in warm water is said to guard against travel sickness. Ginger is believed to be an aid to digestion and to help stimulate the circulation. Ginger was introduced to England before 1066 and was used mainly as a baking spice. Elizabeth I had a fancy for gingerbread which her cook made into the likeness of her courtiers, the prototype for our traditional gingerbread man.

## Quality
Ground Ginger should have a strongly spicy flavour and pale cream colour. Gingerols are the principal flavour constituents.

## Usage
Indian chat masala includes Ground Ginger. This is an unusual sour but fresh tasting spice mix which includes dried Mint. It is used with fruit, vegetables, salads and lentil dishes.
Ginger is one of the warming spices - hence its use with melon to balance a cold food.
Moroccos intriguing spice mix, ras-el-hanout, contains a wide range of spices, amongst them dried Ginger. It is used in traditional tagines, couscous and in almond and honey desserts.
Glaze grilled chicken pieces with Ginger, honey and oil.
Use Ginger in stir-fry dishes to add a spicy warmth.
Sweet potatoes and carrots are delicious sprinkled with Ground Ginger.
Marinade fish with Ginger, sherry, garlic and, for a stronger flavour, Chinese 5 Spice Seasoning, before baking or steaming.
Add ground Ginger to fruit crumble toppings.

HeartCare Healthy Lifestyle Recipes - fourth edition - 2003

**Juniper Berries** *(Juniperus communis)*   Use 6-8 Berries for 4 servings

## Description
Juniper berries are the deep purple fruit of the Juniper bush. They have a bitter sweet, pine flavour with a peppery aftertaste.
Juniper Berries complement - beef, game, pork, venison, cabbage, terrines.

## Did you know?
Juniper Berries can take 3 years to ripen on the bush. Juniper gives its distinctive flavour to gin and other spirits. Cooks in the mountainous regions of Italy, France and Germany use Juniper to flavour rich game dishes.
Although Juniper grows in Britain we do not have many traditional culinary uses for it. However, it adds an excellent flavour to game, pâté and marinades. It is believed to be a diuretic and anti-inflammatory.

## Quality
The berries should be large, round and plump with a deep purple colour and slight dusty bloom.

## Usage
Lightly crush the berries before use to release their flavour.
Add Juniper Berries to rich beef stews and game casseroles.
Pork and venison can be well flavoured with Juniper.
Sauerkraut is traditionally flavoured with Juniper.
Use Juniper in conjunction with herbs, wine and garlic for a full flavour.
Crushed Juniper Berries are good in rich terrines, as well as being used whole with Bay Leaves as a final garnish.

**Mace** *(Myristica fragrans)*     Use 1-2 tsp for 4 servings

### Description
Mace is the scarlet lacy covering which surrounds the hard black shell of the nutmeg. The flavour is aromatic, sweet, warm and rich.

### Did you know?
Nutmegs form a major crop for the island of Grenada, which is often called the Nutmeg Isle. The Nutmeg comes well packaged - first in a hard shell, then covered by the network of Mace and finally with a fleshy outer shell, similar to an apricot. This part of the fruit is used locally for making jam. Connecticut in the USA was known as the Nutmeg State because Yankee peddlars sold whittled wooden Nutmegs to housewives as the genuine spice. Nutmeg can cause hallucinations when eaten in large quantities. In the 18th century, Nutmeg was considered a cure-all.

### Quality
Nutmegs should have a light brown colour and strong aromatic flavour. Schwartz special milling process preserves the flavour - giving volatile oils. Nutmeg is very oily causing the Ground Nutmeg to clump together in the jar. Just shake to loosen before using. Mace has a brighter orange colour and nutmeg-like flavour.

### Usage
Mace adds a sweetness and warmth to both sweet and savoury dishes. Mace has a more delicate flavour for lighter dishes.
Mace is excellent in dishes made with milk and cheese, such as rice pudding, béchamel sauce and whipped cream.
Add Mace to onion confit and vichyssoise as well as pâtés and terrines.

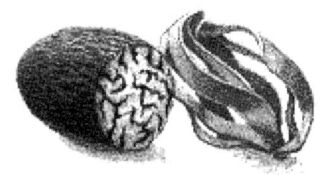

**Mustard Seed**  *(Sinapsis alba)*     Use 1-2 tbs for 4 servings

### Description
Mustard seed has a clean fresh aroma and pungent biting flavour.
Mustard Seed complements - pork, kidneys, veal, rabbit, fish, vegetables, cheese, pickles.
The pungency of Mustard only develops with the addition of water. Heat reduces this pungency and, therefore, to retain the heat it is best to add Mustard towards the end of cooking.

### Did you know?
Mustard has been used as a condiment for thousands of years. For poor people it was the one spice with which they could afford to enliven their bland food.

### Quality
Mustard Seed should have a uniform golden colour with a fresh, sharp flavour. Allyl isothiocyanate is the principal flavour-giving volatile oil.

### Usage
White Mustard is a strong preservative, hence its use in pickles.
Crushed Mustard Seeds go well with vegetables, especially cabbage and celery.
Add Mustard Seed to cheese and cream sauces as well as mayonnaise.
Pork, veal, kidneys and rabbit are all excellent seasoned with Mustard Seed.

**Please visit our web site -  www.heartcarecsg.co.uk**

**Nutmeg** *(Myristica fragrans)*     Use 1-2 tsp for 4 servings

### Description
Nutmeg is the seed of a tropical tree and has an aromatic, sweet, warm and rich flavour.
Nutmeg complements - beef, seafood, veal, vegetables, potatoes, tomato and white sauce, quiches, stewed fruit, biscuits, cakes, milk puddings.

### Did you know?
Nutmegs form a major crop for the island of Grenada, which is often called the Nutmeg Isle. The Nutmeg comes well packaged - first in a hard shell, then covered by the network of Mace and finally with a fleshy outer shell, similar to an apricot. This part of the fruit is used locally for making jam. Connecticut in the USA was known as the Nutmeg State because Yankee peddlars sold whittled wooden Nutmegs to housewives as the genuine spice. Nutmeg can cause hallucinations when eaten in large quantities. In the 18th century, Nutmeg was considered a cure-all.

### Quality
Nutmegs should have a light brown colour and strong aromatic flavour. Schwartz special milling process preserves the flavour - giving volatile oils. Nutmeg is very oily causing the Ground Nutmeg to clump together in the jar. Just shake to loosen before using. Mace has a brighter orange colour and nutmeg-like flavour.

### Usage
Nutmeg adds a sweetness and warmth to both sweet and savoury dishes. Nutmeg is excellent in dishes made with milk and cheese, such as rice pudding, béchamel sauce and whipped cream.
Add Nutmeg to Italian pasta dishes such as Bolognese sauce or stuffings for tortellini, ravioli and cannelloni. Add a subtle difference to the béchamel sauce in lasagne with a pinch of Nutmeg.
Vegetables such as spinach, carrots, mushrooms and sweet potato improve when flavoured with Nutmeg.
Add Nutmeg to onion confit and vichyssoise as well as pâtés and terrines. Greek moussaka and spanakopita (spinach pie) are traditionally spiced with Nutmeg.

**Paprika**  *(Capsicum annuum)*          Use 1-2 tbs for 4 servings

### Description
Paprika is a deep red, slightly earthy flavoured spice made from the dried and ground sweet pepper.
Paprika complements - pork, chicken, veal, vegetables, potatoes, cheese and egg dishes.

### Did you know?
Although related to the hot chilli pepper the cultivation of this plant in the Northern hemisphere has eliminated the capsaicin content which provides the heat in chilli peppers. Paprika was introduced to Hungary by the conquering Turks in 1699. Paprika is a rich source of Vitamin C.

### Quality
Paprika should have a bright red colour and a mild, sweet, earthy aroma. Pungency can vary according to the type.

### Usage
Paprika is the national spice of Hungary and a typical goulash makes an excellent warming winter stew. Paprika also goes well in chicken casseroles. Paprika makes a colourful garnish for mayonnaise, white sauces and creamy soups.
Give Swiss rosti an appetising colour by tossing the grated potato in Paprika before frying.
In Spain Paprika is used in traditional dishes such as zarzuela (a delightful fish stew).
Baharat is a fiery blend of spices from the Gulf States and includes Paprika .
Paprika gives the popular Schwartz Chicken Seasoning its lovely rich colour. Sprinkle over a whole chicken before roasting or onto strips of chicken before stir-frying.

**Pepper** *(Piper nigrum)*    Use 1/2 1 tsp for 4 servings

### Description
Peppercorns are the berries of a tropical vine. They have a warm pungent slightly nutmeg flavour and a hot, biting taste.
To give a spicy flavour and heat, sprinkle into all savoury dishes at the end of cooking or at the table.

### Did you know?
Pepper is known as the 'King of spices', being the most widely used spice in the West. The trade in Pepper and other spices was the major cause of medieval wars and the main reason for world exploration. In the Middle Ages, Peppercorns were even used as currency. Black Peppercorns are the green unripe berries which become black and shrivelled when dried in the sun. To produce White Pepper the outer skin of the ripening berry is removed and the hard core is then dried in the sun. Green Peppercorns are the green berries picked and dried artifically to retain their colour. (Pink Peppercorns are the berries of a tropical bush). Good quality Black Peppercorns will keep for many years. Their warm pungent flavour is released on grinding and is enhanced by heat. However, once ground the volatile oils soon evaporate so add freshly ground Pepper at the table or towards the end of cooking. Green Peppercorns are the world's newest spice, only introduced in 1971. They are milder than black or white. Pepper stimulates the digestive juices, increases the appetite and aids digestion.

### Quality
Black Peppercorns should be large, even in size and a deep rich brown colour. They should be hard and free from stalks and dust.

### Usage
Shake over Ground Black Pepper to add character to casseroles, sauces, egg and cheese dishes.
Serve a salad of roast sweet peppers marinated in olive oil, Garlic, Chilli and Herbes de Provence or Italian Seasoning. Add a dash of lemon juice and Ground Black Pepper.
Bring out the flavour of strawberries with a sprinkling of Ground Black Pepper and a Balsamic vinegar.
Lightly fry a selection of mushrooms in olive oil and butter, pile onto toasted olive ciabatta bread and season well with Ground Black Pepper.

### Saffron *(Crocus sativus)*   Use 1/2 sachet for 4 servings

**Description**
Saffron, the world's most expensive spice, is the dried red stigmas of the autumn-flowering crocus. It has a unique and distinctively pungent, honey-like flavour and aroma.
Saffron complements - rice, chicken, fish, cakes, buns, curries, potatoes, yoghurt, cream.
Use sparingly as a little goes a long way.
For an even flavour and colour, steep a pinch of crushed Saffron strands in a little hot water before adding both to the dish. Add crushed Saffron strands directly to the water when cooking rice.

**Did you know?**
More than 75,000 crocus are needed to produce a pound (450g) of Saffron. The word 'Saffron' comes from the Arabic 'Za'faran' meaning yellow. Saffron Waldon in Essex was so named because of its cultivation of Saffron for over 400 years. The spice has always been expensive and, therefore, open to adulteration. In the Middle Ages, punishment for this crime was extreme. In 1444, a German named Findeker was ordered to be burned at the stake for adulterating Saffron. The use of Saffron in Cornish cooking is believed to have originated from trade with the Phoenicians for Cornish tin.

**Quality**
Saffron can easily be adulterated; there is no such thing as cheap Saffron. The stigmas should be a deep vibrant red colour and have a strong clinging aroma.

**Usage**
Cornish Saffron buns are made with yeast and include currants and candied peel.
Paella, a rice and seafood dish from Spain, is seasoned and coloured with Saffron.
Italian risotto á la Milanese is a deliciously rich and creamy rice dish cooked with Arborio rice, bone marrow, Saffron and Parmesan cheese.
Bouillabaisse, the famous French fish stew, served with creamy aioli and hot rouille sauces, is flavoured with Saffron.
Lamb tagine with dates, a Moroccan dish, is a fragrantly spiced casserole mundane mashed potato with Saffron, Garlic and olive oil, served in the traditional domed dish, with accompanying couscous. Saffron adds a gentle colour and flavour.
A modern recipe enhances mundane mashed potatoes with Saffron, Garlic and virgin olive oil.

### Sesame Seed *(Sesamum indicum)*  Use 2-4 tbs for 4 servings

### Description
Sesame is the nutty flavoured, normally cream coloured, oval seed of the fruit pod of a tropical tree.
Sesame Seeds complement - chicken, stir-fries, dips, bread rolls, biscuits, pastry, salads.

### Did you know?
The password 'Open Sesame' from the tale of Ali Baba was probably inspired by the sharp popping sound and spring-like action of a ripe Sesame pod opening. Sesame Seed is often cultivated for its oil which is excellent in cooking. The Babylonians made cakes, wine and brandy from Sesame Seeds and used the oil for cooking and toiletries. Sesame Seeds are believed to be slightly laxative.

### Quality
Sesame Seeds should be pearly white and even sized with a fresh nutty flavour.

### Usage
To increase the nutty flavour of Sesame Seeds, toast or dry fry them gently until they turn a light golden brown colour.
In the West we use Sesame Seeds mainly as a garnish for bread and cakes. Tahini is a paste of ground Sesame Seeds . Mixed with Garlic and lemon juice it makes a mouth-watering dip for chunks of bread and fresh vegetables.
Sprinkle Sesame Seeds into stir-fries for texture and flavour.
In Tunisia, almond and sesame pastry or samsa is a very sweet dessert made with Sesame Seeds, almonds, sugar, rosewater and lemon.
In the Middle East, samakah harah is a fish dish prepared with a sauce made from crushed Sesame Seeds, Garlic and lemon juice.

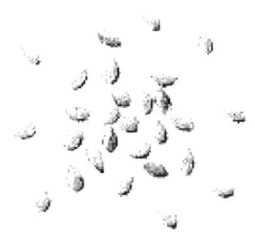

### Turmeric *(Curcuma longa)*     Use 1-2 tsp for 4 servings
### Description
Turmeric adds a brilliant yellow colour and an earthy flavour to foods such as Indian curries, rice and vegetarian dishes.
Turmeric complements - curries, vegetables, rice, fish, eggs, pickles, chutneys, cream sauces.

### Did you know?
Turmeric was used for centuries as a colouring agent, often being substituted for the more expensive Saffron, hence its medieval name 'Indian Saffron'. In Asia it is believed to be a tonic and a remedy for liver problems. In Indonesia rice dyed with Turmeric is traditionally part of the wedding ritual. Turmeric is also used to colour the arms of the bride and groom and to give a golden flush to the cheeks. Today in the West it is used to colour cheese, pickles and mustards.

### Quality
Ground Turmeric should have a brilliant, deep yellow colour and a fresh, pungent, earthy flavour and aroma with ginger and pepper overtones.

### Usage
Use Turmeric wherever a dish will be enchanced by a brighter yellow colouring such as eggs, relishes, mustard or cream sauces, soups and flavoured butter. Piccalilli is probably the best known product in the UK for the use of Turmeric Sprinkled into the cooking water for rice, together with Whole Cloves, a Cinnamon Stick and Cardamom Pods, Turmeric gives rice a beautiful golden colour. Seafood sauces can be enhanced with Turmeric or try a caper sauce for fish with Turmeric, Parsley, Allspice, Bay Leaves, Cloves, cream and capers flavouring a basic béchamel sauce.
Indian Brahmin vegetarian dishes are flavoured with sambhar powder, a hot spicy mix using Turmeric and asafoetida, which balances the 'windy' properties of beans and pulses. Ethiopian beef in pepper sauce mingles the spiciness of Chillies, Garlic and Ginger with the fragrance of Turmeric and Cardamom. Indonesian nasi kunig is a fluffy rice dish flavoured with coconut milk, Lemon Grass and Turmeric.

**Vanilla**  *(Vanilla planifolia)*     Use 1/2-1 vanilla pods for 4 servings

### Description
Vanilla is a long, slender, black seed pod. It has a sweet, slightly smoky aroma and taste and is one of the world's most popular flavourings for sweet dishes. Vanilla complements - cakes, puddings, cream, ice-cream, rice puddings, pancakes, custard.

### Did you know?
The Aztec Indians in Mexico used Vanilla Pods to flavour their chocolate drink Xoco-latl. Vanilla Pods are picked green when they have no scent. The lengthy curing process, which develops Vanillas fragrant aroma, is one reason for its high cost. Good quality Vanilla Pods give an even better flavour than essence and can be re-used many times. Vanilla was believed to be a tonic for the brain.

### Quality
Vanilla Pods should be a rich, deep brown colour, somewhat wrinkled in appearance but still supple and resilient. The complex, but subtle, fruity 'bouquet' develops with age and is long lasting. Vanillin is the primary flavour constituent of vanilla beans.

### Usage
For cakes, puddings and sweets keep a Vanilla Pod in a jar of sugar to be used for baking. Top up with more sugar and the same pod will perfume the added sugar for up to a year.
For sauces, custards and ice-cream, infuse the milk with a Vanilla Pod. Afterwards the pod can be rinsed, dried and returned to an airtight container. The same method can be used for syrups and poached fruit.
For a stronger flavour and authentic texture, the pod can be split open and the tiny black seeds used in the dish.
Flavour the milk for a sweet pancake mixture with Vanilla.
Add a pod to rice pudding mixture and remove after cooking.
French clafouti batter is flavoured with Vanilla. For crème chantilly beat Vanilla sugar into the cream or infuse a few tablespoons of milk with a Vanilla Pod and beat into the cream and sugar.
The milk used to make the custard for a bavarois should be infused with a Vanilla Pod for extra fragrance.
Whilst not generally associated with savoury dishes, Vanilla can add a subtle but unusual new flavour to delicate sauces for fish and seafood.

# Fish

**HeartCare Healthy Lifestyle Recipes - fourth edition - 2003**

*These recipes are ideal for a barbecue on a fine summer day or they can be cooked just as well in the oven.*

*Fresh fish is good for you and tastes delicious. Try to eat oily fish at least twice a week. It is low in unsaturated fat and is high in Omega 3 fatty acids. It is also a rich source of vitamins A and D.*

*Fish is ideal for counting calories, for entertaining and for those on a low cholesterol diet.*

*Try making your own fish stock for a stronger, richer flavour, see page 64.*

## Cod Nicoise

**Ingredients: -**
1 - onion, finely chopped
45ml/3 tbsp - olive oil
¾ lb - tomatoes, skinned and quartered
15ml/1 tbsp - tomato puree
1 - bay leaf or ¼ tsp - ground bay
Pinch salt and black pepper
4 - portions of skinned boned cod
230g/½ lb - carrots, finely chopped
½ - red pepper, chopped small

**Method: -**
Fry onion and diced carrot and half of red pepper in the oil for 10 minutes, until tender.
Add the garlic, then stir in all remaining ingredients, except fish.
Turn into an oven-proof dish.
Arrange the fish on top of the vegetables.
Cover and bake for 1-1½ hours at 150°C/300°F/gas mark 2.

## Fish Crumble

*The following recipe works well with any White fish, or drained canned fish such as Tuna, Salmon or Mackerel. It is also really nice with fresh Mackerel. If there is any excess moisture in the mixture, then add a few fresh breadcrumbs.    Serves 4*

**Ingredients: -**

450g/1lb - smoked cod fillet
30ml/2 tbsp - virgin olive oil
175g/6oz - leeks, sliced
2 - carrots, diced
350g/12oz - closed cup mushrooms, thickly sliced
45ml/3 tbsp - plain flour
250ml/8fl oz - semi-skimmed milk
125g/4oz - double Gloucester cheese, grated
25g/1oz - butter
25g/1oz - medium oat flakes

**Method: -**

Remove the skin from the smoked cod fillet and cut the fish into large cubes.
Heat the oil and cook the leeks and carrots for 2 minutes.
Add the mushrooms and cook for 2 minutes. Stir in the flour and cook for a minute.
Remove from the heat and stir in the milk gradually.
Return to the heat and bring to the boil, stirring.
Stir in three-quarters of the cheese and set aside.
Arrange the fish in a 1 litre/1¾ pint ovenproof dish, then cover with the sauce.
Rub the butter into the oat flakes, stir in the remaining cheese, then sprinkle over the fish and sauce.
Bake in a preheated oven, 190ºC/375ºF/gas mark 5, for about 30 minutes.

# Healthy Seafood Lasagne
Serves 4

**Ingredients: -**
100g/4oz - skinned smoked haddock
100g/4oz - skinned plaice fillets
100g/4oz - peeled prawns
50g/2oz - button mushrooms
25g/1oz - plain flour
225g/8oz - low fat fromage frais
9 sheets - oven ready lasagne verdi
75g/3oz - low fat Cheddar type cheese, grated
3 - unpeeled prawns
300ml/½ pint - skimmed milk
25g/1oz - virgin olive oil
1 - onion
50g/2oz - frozen peas
15ml/1 tbsp - chopped parsley
15ml/1 tbsp - tomato puree
Green pepper slices

**Method: -**
Cut the fish into small bite-sized cubes and put in a pan with the peeled prawns and the milk.
Bring to the boil and simmer for 5 minutes. Drain milk into a jug.
Put oil in a clean saucepan. Peel and finely chop the onion and add to the pan.
Wipe and slice the mushrooms, cook over a gentle heat with the peas and onion for 2-3 minutes.
Stir in the flour, gradually add the reserved milk to make a sauce.
Stir in the chopped parsley and the tomato puree.
Add the fish.
Dip the lasagne in warm water, spoon a little of the fish sauce and filling onto the base of a 1.1 litre/2 pint shallow ovenproof dish.
Arrange 3 sheets of lasagne on top, follow with another 2 layers of filling and lasagne.
Combine the fromage frais with the grated cheese and spread over the lasagne.
Cook for 30 minutes in the oven 180ºC/350ºF/gas mark 4.
Garnish with slices of green pepper and unpeeled prawns.
Serve with hot vegetables or salad.

## Herbed Fish Cakes
Serves 4

**Ingredients: -**
275g/10oz - haddock, skinned and boned
15ml/1 tbsp - Worcestershire sauce
15ml/1 tbsp - creamed horseradish
4 fl ozs/100ml - skimmed milk
15ml/1 tbsp - snipped fresh chives
15ml/1 tbsp - chopped parsley
350g/12oz - cooked and mashed potatoes
50g/2oz - fresh wholemeal breadcrumbs
lemon juice

**Method: -**
Puree fish in food processor or mash with a fork and mix with lemon juice, Worcestershire sauce and horseradish.
Stir in the milk, herbs and potatoes.
Shape mixture into 4 fish cakes and coat with wholemeal breadcrumbs.
Grill under moderate heat for 5 minutes each side, until the cakes are browned.
Serve with hot vegetables or salad.

## Homemade Fish Stock
(This is **not** a soup)

**Ingredients: -**
Bones and trimmings from fish
1 - onion, sliced
2 - carrots, chopped
1 - leek, chopped
6 - peppercorns
900ml/1½ pints - water
300ml/½ pint - white wine
1 - bouquet garni

**Method: -**
Place bones and trimmings from the fish into a saucepan with 900ml/1½ pints of water.
Add the onion, carrots, leek, wine and the bouquet garni to the pan.
Bring gently to the boil and simmer for 30 minutes.
Add 6 peppercorns for the last 10 minutes.
Strain.
Makes 1¼ litres/2 pints.

HeartCare Healthy Lifestyle Recipes - fourth edition - 2003

# Low Fat Fish Bake
### Serves 4

**Ingredients: -**
450g/1lb - haddock or other white fish, skinned and boned
425ml/¾oz - skimmed milk
1 - bay leaf
1 - onion, peeled and chopped
25g/1oz - olive oil or butter
25g/1oz - plain flour
2 x 15ml/2 tbsp - chopped parsley
50g/2oz - mushrooms, sliced
2 - sticks celery, finely sliced

**Topping: -**
450g/1lb - potatoes, peeled, diced and boiled for 2/3 minutes
50g/2oz - Edam or low fat Cheddar type cheese, grated
2 x 15ml/2 tbsp - wholemeal breadcrumbs

**Method: -**
Poach fish in milk with bay leaf and onion for 8/10 minutes.
Strain milk into saucepan, add margarine and flour and bring to the boil whisking continuously and cook for 2/3 minutes.
Add the flaked fish, parsley, mushrooms, celery and mix carefully together.
Place in ovenproof dish.
Pile the potato on top of the fish mixture and sprinkle with cheese and breadcrumbs.
Place in heated oven 190ºC/375ºF/gas mark 5 for 15/20 minutes, until golden brown.
Serve with a green vegetable, such as broccoli, peas or beans.

## Pasta and Salmon Bake
Serves 4

**Ingredients: -**
225g/8oz - wholemeal pasta, any shape
25g/1oz - virgin olive oil
125g/4oz - sliced button mushrooms
198g/1 x 7oz - can of salmon, drained and flaked
125g/4oz - Edam or low fat Cheddar type cheese, grated
75g/3oz - wholemeal breadcrumbs
1 Red - pepper, chopped small
1 x 7oz - can sweet corn, drained - no added salt or sugar
Black pepper

**Method: -**
Cook pasta in boiling water until tender, about 7 minutes - drain.
Boil the red pepper for 4/5 minutes, then drain and chop into small pieces.
Melt the margarine, cook mushrooms until tender.
In a large pan, mix the red pepper, add the cooked mushrooms, sweet corn, salmon and pasta, add 75g/3oz of the cheese.
Toss over a low heat until heated through, add pepper to taste.
Put into ovenproof casserole dish, sprinkle with a mixture of cheese and breadcrumbs and grill until brown.

# Poached Fish with a Lemon Sauce
Serves 4

## Ingredients: -
4 - whiting, cod or other firm white fish fillets
150ml/¼ pint - hot fish stock   (see Stock Tip, page 26)
150ml/¼ pint - skimmed milk
2 - lemons
150ml/¼ pint - low fat natural yoghurt
1 - bouquet garni
15ml/1 tbsp - corn flour
Parsley to garnish

## Method: -
Place the fish fillets in a shallow pan and cover with the hot stock and skimmed milk.
Peel and slice the lemons and add to the fish with the bouquet garni.
Bring slowly to simmering point. Poach the fish for about 5/8 minutes until the fish is cooked.  Remove the fish carefully with a fish slice and keep warm.
Reserve the liquid and discard the bouquet garni.
Blend the natural yoghurt and the corn flour together, add to the poaching liquid and whisk.
Bring to the boil very gently, stirring and simmer for 3 minutes until slightly thickened.
Add a very small knob of low fat spread.
Garnish the fish with parsley.
Serve with new potatoes and green vegetables.

## *Salmon Steaks in Mushroom Sauce*
Cook in Microwave. Serves 4

### Ingredients: -
40g/1½oz - plain flour
600ml/1 pint - milk
1 - bay leaf
blade of mace
25g/1oz - butter or low fat spread
225g/8oz - button mushrooms
4 - salmon steaks

### Garnish:-
Lemon
Parsley

### Method: -
Put the flour in a glass bowl and mix in the milk gradually, first making a smooth paste, then adding it more quickly and whisking all the time.
Add the bay leaf, mace, seasoning and butter.
Cook on high heat for 7-10 minutes until the sauce has boiled and thickened, whisking once halfway through the cooking time.
Add the mushrooms and cook on high heat for a further minute.
Cover and keep warm.
Cook the salmon steaks, covered, on high heat for 8 minutes.
Stand for 5 minutes.
Reheat the sauce for 1-2 minutes and pour around the fish.
Garnish with lemon and parsley.

**Please visit our web site - www.heartcarecsg.co.uk**

## Summer Trout in Foil
Serves 4

**Ingredients: -**
4x250g/8oz - trout, heads and tails removed
Sprig of fresh herbs - parsley, thyme or dill
15ml/1 tbsp - olive oil
15ml/1 tbsp - lemon juice per fish
4 - mushrooms, thinly sliced
4 - tomatoes, thinly sliced
4 - spring onions, chopped
Ground pepper

**Method: -**
Gut the trout, wash and dry.
Sprinkle inside and out with lemon juice.
Place the herbs inside each fish, season with pepper.
Brush four pieces of foil with oil.
Place fish onto foil and add the onions, mushrooms and tomatoes.
Crimp and fold foil to make a well sealed parcel.
To: **oven cook: -** preheat oven 190°C/375°F/gas mark 5. Place parcels on a baking tray and cook for 30 minutes.
To: **barbecue: -** Place on barbecue for approximately 30 minutes.
Serve with a green salad.

# Tuna, Pasta and Broccoli Bake

Preparation: 20 minutes  Cooking: 25 minutes  Serves 4

### Ingredients: -
225g/8oz - pasta twists
175g/6oz - broccoli pieces or florets
400g/14oz - can tuna fish in brine, drained

### Cheese Sauce: -
50g/2oz - sunflower margarine
50g/2oz - wholewheat flour
600ml/1 pint - skimmed milk
75g/3oz - low fat Cheddar type cheese
2.5ml/½ tsp - mustard powder
Black Pepper to season

### Topping: -
25g/1oz - fresh wholemeal bread crumbs

### Method: -
Cook pasta in boiling water for 5 minutes and then add bite-sized broccoli florets.
Return to the boil and cook for another 4-5 minutes until the pasta and broccoli are just tender, drain.
Flake the tuna fish over the bottom of an ovenproof dish.
To make the cheese sauce, put the margarine, flour and milk in a saucepan and heat gently until the margarine has melted.
Turn the heat up and stir continuously until the sauce boils and thickens.
Simmer for 2-3 minutes, then remove from the heat and stir in half of the cheese, mustard and season with pepper.
Arrange the pasta and broccoli over the tuna and cover with sauce.
Mix together the breadcrumbs with the remaining cheese and sprinkle over the top.
Bake in a preheated oven to 200ºC/400ºF/gas mark 6 for about 25 minutes, or until the top is golden and crisp.
Serve with lightly grilled tomatoes.
A packet of cheese sauce mix made up with skimmed milk, could be used to save time.

# Main Course

HeartCare Healthy Lifestyle Recipes - fourth edition - 2003

## *Beef and Mushroom Stew with Parsley Dumplings*
Serves 4 - low fat version

*Beef stew is always more flavoursome if made a day in advance as this allows the flavours to mingle. To do this, make the beef stew and then allow to cool and refrigerate overnight. Next day, skim off any visible fat before reheating. When heated, add the parsley dumplings and cook for the required time.*

**Ingredients for the Stew: -**
500g/1lb - braising or rump steak
250g/8oz - button mushrooms, quartered
3 - medium carrots, peeled and diced
1 - onion, chopped
2 - bay leaves
275ml/½ pint - beef stock
275ml/½ pint - red wine or stout
45ml/3 tbsp - plain flour
45ml/3 tbsp - polyunsaturated oil
dash of Worcester sauce
freshly ground black pepper

**Ingredients for the Dumplings: -**
45ml/3tbsp - self raising flour
40g/1½oz - fresh breadcrumbs
30ml/2tbsp - parsley, chopped

**Method: -**

**Stew: -**
Cut off all visible fat from the beef, cut the beef into 2.5cm/l" cubes.
Put the oil into a pan and sauté the onion until soft - remove the onion and keep to one side.
Put the seasoned flour into a polythene bag and toss the meat in the flour, a few pieces at a time.
Turn up the heat and brown the meat in batches. When brown, remove and set aside.
Return the onion to the pan.
Stir in the wine or stout and the stock, then return the beef back into the pan.
Add the bay leaves, diced carrots, mushrooms and a dash of Worcester sauce.
Cover and simmer for two hours or until the meat is tender.
Discard the bay leaves.

**Dumplings: -**
Mix the dumpling ingredients together and add enough water to form a soft dough.
With floured hands shape into four even sized rounds.
Place the dumplings into the pan, cover and simmer for 15 to 20 minutes.

## Bulgar Wheat Pilaff with Nuts and Seeds
Serves 4

**Ingredients: -**
150g /5 oz - onions, thinly sliced
800ml /1½ pint - vegetable stock
300g /11oz - Bulgar wheat
25g /1 oz - unsalted, raw cashew nuts
25g /1 oz - pumpkin seeds  (rich in healthy omega oils)
15ml/1 tbs - sesame seeds
1 - pomegranate or 1 - dessert apple or 6 - ready to eat apricots
30ml/2 tbs - chopped fresh mint   (great to help with digestion)

**Method: -**
Sauté onions in 30ml/2 tbs of hot stock until softened.
Stir in Bulgar wheat and rest of stock and bring to boil.
Cover and simmer for 12-15 minutes until Bulgar is tender and stock absorbed.
Meanwhile, under hot grill, toast cashew nuts for about 30 seconds until golden.
Dry-fry pumpkin and sesame seeds over medium heat in frying pan until they pop, stirring constantly (as they jump about!)
Stir nuts and seeds into Bulgar wheat. Cut up pomegranate and scoop out seeds and juice, add to wheat. (If not using pomegranate, use chopped raw apple or apricots).
Stir in mint and serve.

## Chicken Curry
Serves 2

**Ingredients: -**
2 - chicken joints with all fat and skin removed
1 x 400g/14oz - can tomatoes
1 - bay leaf
1 - eating apple, cored and chopped small
10ml/2 tsp - Branston pickle (or similar)
5ml/1 tsp - tomato puree
1 - medium onion, finely chopped
1 - tablespoon curry powder

**Method: -**
Place the chicken joints and the remaining ingredients in a saucepan and bring to the boil.
Place a lid on the saucepan and cook slowly, for about 1 hour, stirring occasionally, turning the chicken joints every 15 minutes or so.
If the sauce is too thin, remove the lid and cook on a slightly higher heat until the sauce reduces and thickens.
Serve on a bed of rice.

## Chicken and Garlic Casserole

(The long, slow cooking of the Provincial dish renders the garlic to taste mild, aromatic and sweet) Serves 6

**Ingredients: -**

45ml/3 tbsp - fruity extra virgin olive oil
1 - 1.5k:2k/3½lb:4lb chicken cut into about 10 pieces or equivalent chicken breast pieces
2 - sprigs fresh thyme or 2.5ml/½ tsp dried
2 - sprigs fresh rosemary or 2.5ml/½ tsp dried
2 - sprigs fresh sage or 2.5ml/½ tsp dried
1 - small bunch parsley, chopped
2 - sticks celery, chopped
40 - cloves garlic, peeled but left whole (Yes, **40** - see note below)
Salt and pepper
Good pinch of nutmeg

**Method: -**

Preheat oven 190°C/375°F/gas mark 5.
Pour the oil into ovenproof casserole with tight fitting lid.
Add all the ingredients, mix well, best done with hands.
Place the lid on top, a layer of foil in between will help to make a tight fit.
Place in oven and leave undisturbed for 1½ hours.
Serve immediately.
Traditionally the lid is taken off when everyone is seated at the table so that the first blast of delicious aromas can be enjoyed.
Eat with crusty bread or a good Italian bread.

*When I did some typing for the Ed., I felt sure there was a mistake. No one would use 40 cloves of garlic in one recipe. However I was assured this was correct, so what better way to check than to invite a friend round for dinner?*
*I prepared the dish and yes I did use 40 cloves!*
*What a surprise when we sat down to eat!*
*A pleasant one you will be pleased to hear. So all you folk out there who think there is a zero too many, be brave, you will be pleasantly surprised.*
*(However - anyone you happen to meet the next day will not be too impressed)*

*Garlic is rich in anti-oxidants, helps keep the blood healthy and lowers cholesterol*

HeartCare Healthy Lifestyle Recipes - fourth edition - 2003

## *Chicken with Red Wine and Tarragon*
Serves 4

**Ingredients: -**
4 - skinned chicken portions
45ml/3 tbsp - fresh chopped tarragon
15ml/1 tbsp - olive oil
2 - small, red skinned onions, peeled and thinly sliced
90ml/3fl oz - *crème fraîche*
600ml/1 pint - red wine  (rich in antioxidants)
15ml/1 tbsp - lemon juice
Salt and pepper
Sprigs of tarragon (garnish)

**Method: -**
Put the skinned chicken portions in a shallow dish. Mix together all the remaining ingredients, except the *crème fraîche*, and spoon over the chicken.
Cover and chill for 2 hours.
Set the oven to fairly hot. 200°C/400°/gas mark 6.
Remove the chicken portions from the marinade and transfer to a roasting tin, reserving the marinade until later.
Cook the chicken portions for 45 minutes, until golden brown and cooked.
Meanwhile pour the reserved marinade into a small saucepan, bring to the boil and boil vigorously until the liquid is reduced by half.
Remove from the heat and stir in the *crème fraîche*.
Season to taste.
Serve hot or cold.
Pour sauce over the chicken.
Garnish with sprigs of tarragon (optional).

*Chicken is an excellent form of protein, with a much lower saturated fat content than red meat. It contains useful quantities of vitamin B and some minerals.*
*Although the calorie content of chicken depends largely on how it is cooked, it is still regarded as a low-calorie protein food.*
*For example, 25g/1oz lean roast chicken has 35½ calories, lean roast beef has 48 calories, and lean roast leg of pork has 46¼ calories.*

# Devilled Turkey Drumsticks
Serves 4

**Ingredients: -**
4 - turkey drumsticks, skinned and cooked
30ml/2 tbsp - virgin olive oil
10ml/2 tsp - prepared English mustard
10ml/2 tsp - prepared French mustard
15ml/1 tbsp - tomato ketchup
1.25ml/¼ tsp ground ginger
1.25ml/¼ tsp Cayenne pepper
salt and black pepper to taste

**Method: -**
Mix together the mustards, tomato ketchup, ginger, cayenne, salt and pepper to taste.
Make shallow cuts on the drumsticks on both sides.
Brush them with the margarine or low fat spread, then roll them in the mustard mixture.
Leave to marinate for 30 minutes.
Preheat the grill to moderate.
Grill the drumsticks for 15 minutes, or until they are tender, crisp and brown on all sides.

*Coated with a piquant sauce, devilled turkey drumsticks provide the ideal way of using up leftover turkey, as the wings and breast may be cooked in the same way.*

HeartCare Healthy Lifestyle Recipes - fourth edition - 2003

## *Easy Every Day Chicken Stir Fry*
Serves 4

**Ingredients: -**
460g/1lb - boneless skinless chicken breast
10ml/2 tsp - fresh ginger, finely chopped or 5ml/1 tsp if dried
15ml/1 tbsp - extra virgin olive oil
2 - small garlic cloves
2 - onions, coarsely chopped
2 - carrots, thinly sliced on diagonal
2 - celery sticks, diagonally sliced
½ - red pepper
½ - yellow pepper
230g/8oz - broccoli florets or cauliflower florets (fresh or frozen)
30ml/2 tbsp - hoisin sauce or sherry or soy sauce

**Method: -**
Cut chicken into 2.5cm/l" cubes, in large non stick pan or wok.
Heat oil over high heat, stir fry ginger, garlic and chicken for 3 minutes or until lightly browned.
Add onions, stir fry for 1 minute.
Add carrots, celery, peppers, broccoli and cauliflower florets, stir fry for
4 minutes or until vegetables are tender crisp, adding a spoonful of water, if necessary, to prevent scorching.
Stir in hoisin sauce until mixed.

# Gammon Steak and Orange Sauce

**Ingredients: -**
4 - gammon steaks trimmed of all excess fat
5ml/1 tsp - dried marjoram
225ml/8fl oz - dry white wine
150ml/5fl oz - orange juice
25g/l oz - extra virgin olive oil
25g/loz - flour
1 - orange, peeled and sliced
grated rind of above orange
salt and white pepper to taste

**Method: -**
Preheat grill to moderate.
Rub the steaks with the marjoram then grill for 5 minutes each side.
Put wine and orange juice into a saucepan and bring to the boil.
Remove from heat and set aside.
Melt the margarine in another saucepan - remove from heat and stir in the flour to make a smooth paste.
Gradually stir in the wine and orange juice, whisking if any lumps form.
Add salt and pepper to taste and the orange rind.
Return to heat and bring to boil.
Cook, stirring constantly for 2 to 3 minutes or until sauce is thickened and smooth.
Transfer the gammon steaks to a warmed serving dish.
Pour over sauce and garnish with the orange slices.

HeartCare Healthy Lifestyle Recipes - fourth edition - 2003

# *Glazed Roast Gammon*

Try this for a change from all the turkey you have had over Christmas - serves: 6 to 8

**Ingredients: -**
1·8kg/4lb - gammon joint
150ml/¼pint - fresh orange juice
2 - bay leaves
30m/2tbsp - sunflower oil
45ml/3tbsp - clear honey
2·5ml/½tsp - freshly ground black pepper
2 - oranges, very thinly sliced
12 - cloves

**Method: -**
Preheat the oven to 180ºC/350ºF/Mark 4.
Rinse the gammon joint and pat dry with absorbent kitchen paper.
Lift into a roasting tin and pour the orange juice over.
Add the bay leaves, cover tightly with foil and roast for 1 hour 45 minutes.
Mix together the sunflower oil, honey and freshly ground black pepper.
Remove the gammon from the oven.
Take the foil off and arrange orange slices over the skin.
Stud each orange slice with a clove to hold them in place.
Brush the honey mixture over the top liberally.
Return to the oven for 30 minutes, until the topping is golden brown.
Serve the gammon warm with a selection of freshly cooked vegetables, or cold with a salad.
(You can freeze this for up to three months).

# Grilled Chicken with Soy Sauce

(This is an adaptation of a Japanese dish and can be served either as part of a Japanese meal, or as a tempting appetizer)  Serves 4

## Ingredients: -
4 - whole chicken breasts, skinned
125ml/4fl oz - sake or dry sherry
50ml/2fl oz - soy sauce
125ml/¼ oz - chicken stock, skimmed of all fat
10ml/2 tsp - cornflour
2 - celery stalks, thinly sliced into sticks
8 - spring onions

## Method: -
Warm the sake or sherry in a small saucepan.
Remove from the heat, then ignite the sake or sherry with a match.
Allow it to burn until the flames die down.
Stir in the soy sauce and chicken stock.
Dissolve the sugar and cornflour in 45ml/3 tbsp of the soy sauce mixture.
Pour the remaining soy sauce mixture into a shallow dish.
Preheat the grill to moderately high.
Coat the chicken breasts on one side in the soy sauce mixture, then grill until they are golden brown on that side.
Remove from the heat, coat the other side in the soy sauce mixture and return to the grill to cook the second side until it is golden brown.
Remove from the heat and coat the chicken breasts again with the soy sauce mixture.
Place on the grill rack and brush them generously with the soy sauce and cornflour mixture.  Cook for a further 6 minutes by which time they should be a deep golden brown.
Transfer the chicken to warmed serving dishes and garnish with the celery and spring onions.

## Healthy Chicken Casserole
Serves 4

**Ingredients: -**
2 - Chicken portions, skinned
1 - onion peeled and sliced
3 rashers - lean back bacon, fat cut off, chopped
300ml/½ pint - chicken stock or chicken stock cube
12cm/5" - piece of cucumber, diced
30ml/2 tbsp - olive oil
black pepper
20ml/1½ tbsp - plain flour
15ml/1 tbsp - lemon juice

**Method: -**
Heat the olive and sunflower oil in frying pan and brown the skinned chicken both sides. Remove from the pan.
Cook sliced onion and chopped bacon in pan until lightly browned. Stir in the plain flour and cook for 1 minute then gradually stir in the stock.
Bring to the boil, stirring.
Season to taste and add pepper and lemon juice.
Replace chicken into the pan, add the diced cucumber, cover and simmer for about 30 minutes.
Alternatively transfer to an oven proof casserole dish and cook in a preheated oven for 30/40 minutes at oven temperature 180ºC/350ºF/gas mark 4.
Adjust seasoning and serve.

HeartCare Healthy Lifestyle Recipes - fourth edition - 2003

## *Lamb with Red Capsicum Sauce  Serves 4*
(Preparation time - 20 minutes; total cooking time - 40 minutes;

**Ingredients: -**
2 - red capsicums
3 - medium tomatoes, cored
1.25ml/¼ tsp - ground cumin
5ml/1 tsp - ground coriander
5ml/1 tsp - chopped chilli
freshly ground pepper to taste
10ml/2 tsp - chopped mint (preferably fresh)
1 - clove garlic (optional)
4 - lamb steaks, trimmed of all fat
fresh coriander leaves for serving

**Method: -**
Preheat oven to 240°C/475°F/gas mark 9
Place capsicums on oven shelf and bake for 15 minutes.
Add tomatoes and cook for a further 10 minutes.
When cool enough to handle remove blackened skin from capsicums and tomatoes.
Place flesh in blender or processor, add cumin, coriander, chilli, pepper, mint and garlic.
Process until smooth and set aside.
Grill lamb steaks as preferred.
Place some roasted capsicum sauce on each plate, top with a grilled lamb steak.
Add a few sprigs of fresh coriander.
Serve with your favourite vegetable or salad.

## *Lemon Sesame Chicken*

serves four - Preparation time: 20 minutes Cooking time : 50 minutes
This recipe is reprinted from the Somerfield Magazine with their kind permission.

**Ingredients: -**
8 - Somerfield chicken drumsticks or 4 chicken quarters
8 - potatoes, peeled, halved, slits cut in the top
2 - red onions, peeled and cut into wedges
30ml/2 tbsp - Somerfield olive oil
juice and rind of 2 lemons
30ml/2 tbsp - Somerfield clear honey
30ml/2 tbsp - sesame seeds

**Method: -**
Preheat oven to 200°C/400°F/Mark 6.
Pre-boil the potatoes for approximately 10 minutes, drain.
Place the chicken in a large roasting tin, place the potatoes and onion wedges amongst the chicken.
Mix together the oil, lemon juice and rind, pour over the chicken.
Cook for 35 minutes, turning and basting occasionally.
Pour the honey and sesame seeds over the chicken and cook for a further 15 minutes until golden.
Serve with the lemon juice.
Approximate cost £1.00; 620 kcals; Fat 18g.

HeartCare Healthy Lifestyle Recipes - fourth edition - 2003

# *Mushroom Stuffed Chicken*

**Ingredients: -**
1.6kg/3lb chicken
Virgin olive oil

**For the Stuffing: -**
25g/1oz - low fat spread
1 - small onion, finely chopped
175g/6oz - closed cup mushrooms, very finely chopped
1 - clove garlic, crushed
50g/2oz - jasmine rice, cooked and drained
grated rind and juice of ½ lime

**NB: -** The stuffing ingredients can be doubled to stuff a 4.5kg/10lb turkey

**Method: -**
Melt the butter and cook the onion and mushrooms for 3 minutes.
Stir in the garlic and cook for 30 seconds.
Turn into a mixing bowl with the lime rind and juice, rice and seasoning. Leave to cool.
Meanwhile, wipe the chicken all over with absorbent kitchen paper.
Then, beginning at the neck end, insert your hands very carefully between the skin and the breast of the bird and ease the skin away from the breast slowly.
Use about ¾ of the stuffing to form an even layer between the skin and the flesh of the chicken.
Use the remainder to fill the neck end. Secure the neck flap with skewers or string.
Weigh the stuffed chicken and calculate the cooking time.
Brush the chicken lightly with oil and season.
Put into a roasting tin and bake in a preheated oven, 190ºC/375ºF/ gas mark 5, for 20 minutes per 450g/llb, plus 20 minutes.
If the stuffing appears to be over-browning, cover the chicken with a sheet of wet greaseproof paper.

## *Petit Pois with Onions*

(A classic vegetable dish from France that can be served with meat or fish meals. Serves 6.)

**Ingredients: -**
700g/1½lb - petit pois (small peas), fresh and weighed after shelling, or frozen and thawed
2 tsp - sugar
Salt and black pepper
50g/2oz - polyunsaturated margarine
4 - small onions, blanched and halved
2 - shallots, blanched and thinly sliced
4 - spring onions (scallions), blanched and cut into ½ cm/¼" pieces

**Method: -**
Cook the peas, with the sugar, in boiling salted water for 4 minutes or until they are nearly tender.
Drain well and set aside.
Melt the margarine in a saucepan.
Add the onions, shallots and spring onions (scallions) with salt and pepper to taste.
Fry until the onions are golden brown.
Stir in the peas and cook gently for 3 to 4 minutes or until the peas are tender.
Turn into a warmed vegetable dish and serve immediately.

## *Pie or Flan Case*

(Here is a recipe for a traditional pie or flan case without saturated fat)

**Ingredients: -**
1 - cup sifted plain flour
⅓ - cup light syrup
2.75ml/¾ tsp - salt (optional)
30ml/2 tbsp - skimmed milk

**Method: -**
Preheat oven to 240ºC/475ºF/gas mark 9.
Mix the flour and salt in a bowl. Combine the syrup and milk, add all at once to the flour mixture.
Stir with a fork until thoroughly mixed.
Shape the mixture into a ball and place it between two squares of greaseproof paper lightly dusted with flour.
Roll the pastry into a circle large enough to line the pie or flan case.
Arrange pastry in the dish, cut off edges with a knife and press with a fork.
Prick the bottom all over with a fork.
Bake for about 10 minutes or until golden brown.
Cool before adding the filling of your choice.

HeartCare Healthy Lifestyle Recipes - fourth edition - 2003

## *Pizza*

500 k/cals per serving : Serves 4

**Ingredients: -**
**Scone Dough**
225g/8oz - self-raising flour (white or wholemeal)
45ml/1½ fl oz - extra virgin olive oil
150ml/¼ pint - skimmed milk

**Topping**
225g/8oz - grated cheese preferably Mozzarella or Edam
2.5ml/½ tsp - mixed Italian herbs
4 - tomatoes, sliced and skinned or tinned
Anchovy fillets or black olives (optional)

**Method: -**
Preheat oven to 200ºC/400ºF/gas mark 6.
Sift together flour and salt, rub in the margarine and bind with milk to form a soft dough.
Roll out on a greased baking tray or pizza plate.
Mix cheese and herbs and cover dough in layers of cheese and tomatoes.
Finish with a layer of cheese.
Decorate with a lattice of anchovy fillets and stud with black olives.
Bake for 30 minutes.

**Please visit our web site -  www.heartcarecsg.co.uk**

## Pork cooked in Cider, Apples and Peppers

**Ingredients: -**
600g/1lb 6oz - lean pork, 12mm/½" thick slices
2 - small onions, chopped
4 - eating apples
1 - red pepper, de-seeded and cut into thin slices
1 - green pepper, de-seeded and cut into thin slices
468ml/1 pint - medium sweet cider
300ml/½ pint water
30ml/2 tbsp - sunflower oil
15ml/1 tbsp - plain flour
10ml/2 tsp - salt
10ml/2 tsp - ground pepper

**Method: -**
Heat the sunflower oil in a frying pan and lightly fry the onions until golden brown, place in a casserole dish.
Lightly fry the pork in the same oil until slightly brown on each side and place in the casserole dish.
Add flour, salt, pepper to the remaining juices in the frying pan, stirring all the time to make a roux.
Slowly add the cider, stirring all the time.
Pour over the pork and onions.
Top up the liquid with water.
Add the apples and peppers.
Cover casserole dish and bake at 170°C/325°F/gas mk 3 for about 2 hours or until the pork is tender.
Serve hot.
Accompany with carrot sticks, cauliflower.
Nice with new potatoes.

## Red Peppers Roasted with Cherry Tomatoes
Serves 3 - 6

**Ingredients: -**
3 - red peppers
350g/12oz - cherry tomatoes
15ml/3 tsp - runny honey
Olive oil
Sea salt
Freshly ground black pepper

**Method: -**
Cut peppers in half from stem to base, leaving green stalk.
Remove seeds and pith.
Halve cherry tomatoes and fill pepper cavities with these.
Place on a baking tray, drizzle over the honey and a little oil, season with salt and pepper.
Bake in very hot oven for 20 - 30 minutes until peppers are wilted and patched with brown.
Serve garnished with parsley and plenty of good bread.

## Roast Potatoes with Lemon and Rosemary
Serves 4 - 6

**Ingredients: -**
24 - small potatoes or potato pieces, peeled or scrubbed
300ml/½ pint - olive oil
4 - cloves garlic, crushed
Juice and grated rind of 3 lemons
Bunch rosemary, leaves removed from stalks
Salt and freshly ground black pepper

**Method: -**
Preheat oven to 200°C/400°F/gas mark 6.
Boil potatoes for 3 minutes, drain.
Combine rest of ingredients and add to pan.
Put on lid and shake gently until most of the liquid is absorbed.
Place in a roasting dish and roast for 30-40 minutes until crisp and golden.
Serve.

HeartCare Healthy Lifestyle Recipes - fourth edition - 2003

## *Savoury Jacket Potatoes*
Serves 4

**Ingredients: -**
4 - large cooked, hot Jacket potatoes
90ml/6 tbsp - skimmed milk
45ml/3 tbsp - low calorie mayonnaise or low fat live yoghurt
15ml/1 tbsp - chopped chives
2.5ml/½ tsp - paprika
1.25ml/¼ tsp - ground black pepper
225g/8oz - skinned cooked chicken, cut into small pieces
1 - stick celery, thinly sliced
Slices of tomato for garnish

**Method: -**
Cut the cooked potatoes in half lengthways, scoop out the flesh, leaving the skin intact.
Mash the potato with the milk, mayonnaise, chives, paprika and pepper.
Stir in the chicken and celery.
Spoon back into the potato skins and cook until golden brown.
Cooking time: approx 15/20 minutes.
Serve with salad.

## *Southern non-Fried Chicken*
(Oven baked but tastes as if it has been fried) - Serves 4

**Ingredients: -**
4 - chicken portions
7.5ml/1½ tsp - garlic salt  )
7.5ml/1½ tsp - celery salt  )
75ml/5 tbsp - low fat live yoghurt
85g/3oz - flour
5ml/1 tsp - cinnamon
5ml/1 tsp - black pepper

> *These contain salt, which can raise blood pressure in some susceptible people. I have left them as they were in previous issues of this recipe book. It is suggested that you reduce the amount or leave out all together.*

**Method: -**
Skin the chicken portions.
Put the flour, garlic salt, celery salt, cinnamon and black pepper into a plastic bag and mix together.
Put the yoghurt into a dish and coat the chicken portions, one at a time, with the yoghurt. Then put each chicken portion in turn into the season mixture.
When coated, put onto a lightly oiled baking tray and bake in the oven for approximately 35 minutes, depending on the thickness of the chicken.
Oven temperature 180°C/350°F/gas mark 4.

HeartCare Healthy Lifestyle Recipes - fourth edition - 2003

# Spiced Lamb and Beef Risotto
Serves 4

**Ingredients: -**
450g/1lb - shoulder of lamb
1 - clove garlic, crushed
100g/4oz - brown sauce
100g/4oz - peas
1 - onion, chopped
300ml/½ pint - chicken stock
2 - carrots, diced
4 tbsp - chopped parsley or mint
2 x 225g/8oz - cans curried baked beans
Salt and freshly ground black pepper
50g/2oz - rice or brown basamati

**Method: -**
Cut the meat into small pieces, removing and discarding any excess fat.
Place the meat in a large saucepan with the onion and garlic and heat gently until the fat begins to run, pour off excess fat.
Increase the temperature and cook, stirring all the time, until the meat colours and the onion softens.
Add the stock, brown sauce and rice and simmer gently for 30 minutes, adding more stock if the rice looks as though it is going to burn.
Add the carrots, peas, curried beans and parsley or mint. Stir well and cook for a further 10 minutes or until the meat is tender and the rice is cooked.
Adjust seasoning to taste and serve.

*Both onion and garlic have been shown to have cholesterol lowering properties and are good for the heart.*

## Stuffed Red Peppers
Serves 4

### Ingredients: -
4 - large red peppers cut in half and de-seeded
225g/8oz - cooked long grain rice
10ml/2 tsp - virgin olive oil
2 - cloves garlic, crushed
2 - onions, peeled and chopped
400g/14oz - can tomatoes
45ml/3 tbsp - tomato puree
30ml/2 tbsp - chopped fresh parsley
15/ml/1 tbsp - chopped fresh thyme
60ml/4 tbsp - red wine
75g/3oz - cashew nuts
Ground black pepper

### Method: -
Bring a large pan of water to the boil, part-boil the peppers for 5 minutes, drain and cool quickly.
Put the halves of pepper into a large lightly greased ovenproof dish.
Heat the olive oil in a large non-stick pan and fry the onions until soft, add the garlic and cook for 2 minutes.
Add the remaining ingredients, except the rice, and simmer for 20 minutes.
Add the rice and thoroughly mix.
Stuff the peppers with the mixture.
Any left over mixture can be put in the dish around the peppers.
Cook for 25 minutes at 180ºC/350ºF/gas mark 4.

HeartCare Healthy Lifestyle Recipes - fourth edition - 2003

# Sweet and Sour Turkey
Low fat - Serves 4

**Ingredients: -**
450g/1lb - cooked diced turkey
2 - medium carrots, peeled and cut into 12mm/½" strips
1 -Cucumber, cut lengthways 10mm/⅜" strips
1 - onion, cut into wedges
440g can - pineapple rings (cut into pieces)
75g/3oz - sliced mushrooms

**Method: -**
Mix ingredients together in a casserole, place in a microwave oven for a full 20 minutes, or conventional oven for 1 hour on medium.
Take: - 15ml/1 tbsp cornflour, 30ml/2 tbsp vinegar, 15ml/1 tbsp soy sauce (dark), mix together and add to the casserole.
Microwave on **full** for 3 minutes, or place in moderate oven for 5/10 minutes.

## Vegetable Curry
Serves 4

**Ingredients:**
15ml/½ tbsp - virgin olive oil
2 - cloves garlic, peeled and crushed
15ml/½ tbsp - turmeric
15ml/½ tbsp - ground cumin
⅓ - cauliflower, broken into small florets
100g/4oz - carrots, diced
300ml/½ pint - water or stock
½ - large onion, chopped
1.2ml/¼ tsp - chilli powder
2.5ml/½ tsp - ground ginger
300g/12 oz potatoes, peeled and diced
100g/4 oz - red lentils
225-300g/9-12 oz - rice, cooked
2.5ml/½ tsp - coriander

**Method: -**
Heat the oil in a large saucepan and cook onion until transparent, add the garlic and all the spices.
Cook for 1 minute to release the flavours.
Add the cauliflower, carrots, potatoes, lentils and water or stock.
Add extra water if necessary.
Cover the pan and simmer for 30 minutes until vegetables are cooked.
Serve with rice.
You may substitute other vegetables: courgettes, peppers, tomatoes, swede, beans or peas.
This curry is quite mild, if you like it hotter, then add extra spices.

*Vegetables are useful sources of vitamins, fibre and minerals, but the amount of nutrients they provide will vary according to their freshness.*
*It is important to know that many vitamins contained in vegetables, vitamin C in particular, are water-soluble. This means that they not only dissolve during the cooking process, but also if the vegetables are immersed in cold water for too long. It is better nutritionally to quickly rinse and chop before they go into the pot, rather than to prepare them in advance and leaving them to soak.*

HeartCare Healthy Lifestyle Recipes - fourth edition - 2003

## Vegetable Pilaff
(serves 4)

**Ingredients: -**
350g/12oz - long-grain rice
900ml/1½ pints - water
50g/2oz - low fat spread
1 - onion, finely chopped
2 - tomatoes, peeled and chopped
1 - red pepper, pith and seeds removed and finely chopped
2 - celery stalks, finely chopped
125g/4oz - broccoli, chopped
125g/4oz - mushrooms, finely chopped
¼ tsp - cayenne pepper
Salt to taste

*A colourful dish of savoury rice. Vegetable Pilaff comes from West Africa.*

**Method: -**
Put the rice in a saucepan with the water and 1 teaspoon salt.
Bring to the boil, then cover and simmer for 15 to 20 minutes or until the rice is tender and all the liquid has been absorbed.
Remove from the heat.
Set aside and keep hot.
Melt the low fat spread in a frying-pan.
Add the onion and fry until it is soft but not brown.
Stir in the tomatoes, red pepper, celery and broccoli and cook, stirring frequently for 10 minutes or until the vegetables begin to soften.
Stir in the mushrooms and cook for a further 3 minutes.
Season with the cayenne and salt to taste.
Add the rice and stir well.
Cook for 10 minutes to reheat the rice thoroughly.

## Vegetarian Nut Roast
Serves 2

**Ingredients: -**
75g/3oz - nuts, finely ground
50gr/2oz - brown breadcrumbs
1 - small onion, finely chopped
2 - tomatoes, chopped and skinned
2½ml/½ teaspoon - marmite
1 - beaten egg

**Method: -**
Fry the onion and tomatoes
Add to the rest of the ingredients and place in a greased dish.
Cook at 190ºC/375ºF/mark 5 for 35 minutes or until well browned.

HeartCare Healthy Lifestyle Recipes - fourth edition - 2003

# *Wholemeal Asparagus or Vegetable Flan*
(Serves 4 approx 250 calories per serving)

**Ingredients: -**
**For the pastry**
175g/6 oz - wholemeal flour
45ml/3 tbsp - skimmed milk powder
Water to mix

**For the filling**
8 oz - cooked fresh or tinned Asparagus, celery or other vegetables
1 - egg
150ml/¼ - pint skimmed milk
15ml/1 tbsp - wholemeal flour
50g/2oz - mushrooms, thinly sliced
1 - tomato, thinly sliced
15ml/1 tbsp - chopped parsley
Black pepper

**Method: -**
Preheat oven to 190ºC/375ºF/gas mark 5.
To make pastry, mix together the flour and skimmed milk powder. Add enough water to form a dough.
Roll out pastry and line an 20cm/8" greased flan ring. Prick the base, line with foil and fill with dry beans. Bake blind for 10 minutes.
Remove the foil and beans and bake for a further 5 minutes to dry the pastry case.
Chop the asparagus or other vegetables and place in the flan case.
Beat together the egg and milk. Stir in the parsley, pepper and flour.
Pour over the vegetables and arrange mushrooms and tomato slices.
Bake for 30 - 35 minutes until the filling is set.
Serve hot or cold.

HeartCare Healthy Lifestyle Recipes - fourth edition - 2003

# Desserts

**Please visit our web site - www.heartcarecsg.co.uk**

## *All about Fromage Frais*

It looks and tastes like yoghurt, but did you know that fromage frais is really a cheese?
The name is French and it means "fresh cheese".
That is why you will find it with the cheese in the supermarket chill cabinet.
It is made by adding an acid producing culture to warm, pasteurised, skimmed milk, which causes the milk to curdle.
The curd is separated from the whey; poured into tubs and chilled.
English fromage frais is on sale too and looks and tastes just as good.
For a low calorie alternative to mayonnaise in dressings and sandwiches, look for virtually fat-free fromage frais - one tablespoon of mayonnaise has 115 calories; fromage frais contains just 15 calories.
You can use it instead of cream in desserts and pasta sauces and it is a good topping for fruit and muesli snacks.
You can buy fruit flavoured fromage frais which is high in protein and rich in calcium, so it makes a healthy dessert.
In a very low-fat fromage frais, there is only 0.2 g of fat in every 100g.
Flavour fromage frais with snipped chives, curry paste or chilli sauce for a low calorie dressing.

HeartCare Healthy Lifestyle Recipes - fourth edition - 2003

## *Apple Crumble*
Serves 4 - high fibre, with oats and wholemeal flour and low sugar content

**Ingredients: -**
570g/1½lb - apples, peeled, cored and sliced, toss in lemon juice to keep white
60g/2oz - wholemeal flour
60g/2oz - oats (oats are great for lowering cholesterol)
30g/1oz - chopped walnuts
60g/2oz - brown sugar
60g/2oz - low fat spread

**Method: -**
Put the prepared fruit into an oven-proof dish.
Mix together the flour, oats and rub in the low fat spread, until it looks like breadcrumbs.
Stir in the sugar and the nuts and spoon over the fruit.
Bake in a pre-heated oven 180ºC/350ºF/gas mark 4 for 25/30 minutes or until fruit is tender.
Serve with low fat live yoghurt or custard made with skimmed milk.

## *Amazing Sugarless Fatless Cake*

**Ingredients: -**
230g/8oz - cooking dates, not sugar rolled
300ml/10oz - water
450g/1lb - mixed dried fruit
175g/6oz - plain wholemeal flour
45ml/3 tbsp - baking powder
15ml/1 tbsp - carob powder (from health food shop)
5ml/1 tsp - mixed spice
60ml/4 tbsp - orange juice
25g/1oz - ground almonds
grated rind of one orange or lemon
a few flaked almonds for top

**Method: -**
Set oven at 160ºC/325ºF/gas mark 3.
Grease 900litre/2lb loaf tin and line with greaseproof paper and grease the paper that will touch the cake mixture.
Put the dates and water into a saucepan and heat gently.
Remove from the heat and mash the dates.
Add all other ingredients and mix well.
Spoon the mixture into the tin and sprinkle the almonds on the top.
Bake for 1½ hours.

HeartCare Healthy Lifestyle Recipes - fourth edition - 2003

## Banana Cake
Serves 4 - high fibre - makes 1 cake

**Ingredients: -**
500g/1lb - ripe bananas, mashed (about 3 large ones)
40g/1½ oz - chopped walnuts
¾ cup - sunflower oil
90g/3½ oz - sultanas
75g/2½ oz - rolled oats
150g/5 oz - whole wheat flour
10ml/2 tsp - baking powder
¼ cup - sugar

**Method: -**
Mix all ingredients in a bowl.
Spread into a greased and paper lined loaf tin.
Bake in a moderate oven, 180ºC/350ºF/gas mark 4, for 1 hour or until a skewer inserted into centre comes out clean.
Cool for 10 minutes before turning out onto a wire rack to cool completely.

## Bran and Raisin Muffins
Makes 9 or 10

**Ingredients: -**
250g/8oz - wholemeal flour
15ml/3 tsp - baking powder
125g/4oz - soft brown sugar
1 egg - size 3
90ml/6 tbsp - sunflower oil
125g/4oz - bran flakes
125g/4oz - seedless raisins
300ml/½ pint - skimmed milk
Pinch of salt
Large paper muffin cases; grease well if using deep muffin or bun tins

**Method: -**
Pre-heat oven to 200ºC/400ºF/gas mark 6.
Place the flour, baking powder, salt and sugar in a mixing bowl, mix well.
Stir in bran flakes and raisins.
Beat the egg, milk and oil together, then stir into mixture all at once.
Stir just until well mixed. Do not over-mix once fruit has been added.
Spoon straight into muffin cases, filling each two-thirds full.
Bake for 15/20 minutes, or until well risen.
Allow to cool in the tins for 2 minutes, then turn out on a wire rack.
Serve muffins while still warm.

HeartCare Healthy Lifestyle Recipes - fourth edition - 2003

# *Chocolate Surprise Dessert*

serves 4 - low fat - this recipe has no egg yolks and no margarine

## Ingredients: -

**For the crumb crust**
150g/5oz - Amaretti biscuits, flaked
1 - egg white, lightly beaten
Grated rind of 1 orange and some almonds, to decorate

**For the filling**
60ml/4 tbsp - low fat unsweetened cocoa powder
60ml/4 tbsp - caster sugar
350ml/¾ pint - skimmed milk
Preheat oven to 180ºC/350ºF/gas mark 4
Put the biscuits into a polythene bag and crush coarsely with a rolling pin
Reserve 15ml/1 tbsp for the decoration
Tiny pinch of salt

## Method: -

Stir the crumbs into the egg white and toss until well mixed.
Spoon the biscuit mix into a 25cm/10" non-stick round flan tin.
With the back of the spoon, spread the mix evenly over the bottom and up the sides.
Bake for 7-10 minutes, cool in the tin on a wire rack.

# Date & Walnut Bread
Serves 4  High fibre

*Dates and Walnuts and Cottage cheese make a light moist semi-sweet bread cake. This can be eaten plain or lightly spread with honey or even a very low fat cheese spread.*

**Ingredients: -**
225g/½lb - semi-dried dates
225g/½lb - wholemeal flour
150ml/¼oz - skimmed milk
75g/3oz - low fat cottage cheese
45ml/3oz - chopped walnuts
1 egg - beaten
½ tsp - bicarbonate of soda
freshly grated nutmeg
pinch of salt

**Method: -**
Heat the oven to 180°C/350°F/gas mark 4.
Stone and chop the dates.
Put the dates and walnuts into a bowl with the flour and add the nutmeg, salt and bicarbonate of soda. Make a well in the centre.
Rub the cheese through a sieve or strainer, and gradually beat in the egg.
Pour this mixture and the skimmed milk into the flour and mix ingredients together.
Put into a greased 450g/1lb loaf tin and smooth on top.
Bake the loaf for 1 hour and then turn out onto a wire rack to cool.
Cooking time approximately 1 hour.
Although this recipe contains one egg, the amount in each slice is very small.

## Easy Summer Pudding
Serves 4

**Ingredients: -**
6 - large slices of wholemeal bread
100g/4oz - sugar
750g/1½lb - soft summer fruits (either raspberries, strawberries, stoned cherries, blackcurrants or redcurrants or a mixture)

**Method: -**
Remove the crusts from the bread and cut the slices into neat fingers.
Put the sugar and 75 ml/5 tbsp water into a pan and heat slowly, stirring until the sugar dissolves.
Add the fruit and simmer gently for about 7-10 minutes.
Line the base and sides of a 1 litre/2 pint pudding basin with bread fingers.
Add half the hot fruit mixture, cover with bread fingers, add more fruit mixture and cover with more bread.
Cover with a saucer or plate. Put a heavy weight on top.
Refrigerate overnight.
Turn out pudding onto a plate.
Decorate with fresh fruit and serve with fromage frais.

## Edna's Coconut Loaf

**Ingredients: -**
50g/2oz - coconut
150ml/¼ pint - milk
100g/4oz - margarine or low fat alternative
225g/8oz - caster sugar
225g/8oz - self raising flour
2 - large eggs, well beaten

**Method: -**
Soak the coconut in the milk for two hours.
Cream margarine or low fat alternative and sugar together, gradually add the eggs beating well.
Fold in flour, mix in coconut and milk until it forms a dropping consistency. A little more milk may be required.
Line a well greased 2lb loaf tin, pre-heat oven to 180°C/350°F/gas mk 4.
Pour mixture into loaf tin and bake for ¾ to 1 hour until risen and golden, (to check if cooked, insert a small pointed knife into the top until it come away clean).

HeartCare Healthy Lifestyle Recipes - fourth edition - 2003

# Fresh Orange Ring

Cholesterol free i.e. No egg yolks or animal fats.
*Fresh orange juice is whisked into the mixture to make a light fruity sponge which is topped with orange segments and glace icing.*
*Cuts into ten - 195 calories per slice - 44g carbohydrate per slice*

**Ingredients: -**
5 - egg whites
175g/6oz - caster sugar
225g/8oz - plain flour
15ml/3 tsp - baking powder
½ lemon - juice only
1 large orange - grated, rind and juice
pinch of salt

**Method: -**
Whisk the egg whites with the sugar to make a stiff, glossy meringue.
Sift together the flour, salt and baking powder.
Pour the lemon juice into a measuring jug then add enough of the orange juice to make 175ml/6oz.
Stir in a teaspoon of the orange rind. Reserve the remaining juice and rind.
Fold a little of the flour, then a little of the fruit juice alternately into the egg white mixture until they are both evenly incorporated.
Pour into a 1½ pint oiled ring mould then bake at 180ºC /350ºF/gas mark 4 for 30-40 minutes or until well risen and firm to the touch.
Cool in tin for 10 minutes and then turn out into a wire rack.

**For the Decoration: -**
2 oranges - peeled and sliced into segments
50g/2oz - icing sugar

**To decorate: -**
Arrange the orange segments neatly round the top of the cake.
Mix enough of the remaining orange juice into the icing sugar to make a glacé icing that is stiff enough to hold its shape.

HeartCare Healthy Lifestyle Recipes - fourth edition - 2003

## Fruit Cake - Egg Free Recipe

**Ingredients: -**
225g/8oz - currants
175g/6oz - glace cherries chopped
125g/4oz - light brown sugar
175g/6oz - self raising flour
125g/4oz - self raising wholemeal flour
200ml/7oz - cold tea
10ml/1 tsp - ground cinnamon
5ml/1 tsp - grated nutmeg
125g/4oz - mixed chopped nuts
75ml/5 tbsp - sunflower oil
50g/2oz - blanched almonds
30ml/2 tbsp - glace cherries
18cm/7" - non-stick cake tin
grated rind & juice of 1 orange

**Method: -**
Preheat oven to 160ºC/325ºF/gas mark 3.
Mix currants, 125g/4oz cherries, sugar and orange rind in a pan.
Make up the orange juice to 250ml/8oz with tea, then add to the pan.
Bring to the boil, then set aside and cover, leave for 30 minutes.
Mix flours, spices and nuts in a bowl. Make a well in the centre and add the fruit with the liquid and oil.
Beat well and turn into a tin.
Top with almonds and cherries.
Bake for about 1 hour and 20 minutes until a skewer comes out clean.
Cool on a wire rack.
This cake will keep fresh for about two weeks in a sealed tin.

## *Healthy Low-fat Apple Pie made with Potato Pastry*
Serves 4

**Ingredients: -**

**Pastry: -**
175g/6oz - cooked mashed potato
175g/6oz - plain flour
50g/2oz - caster sugar
2.5ml/½ tsp - baking powder

**Filling: -**
2 - large cooking apples
1.25ml/¼ tsp - ground cinnamon, optional
50g/2oz - raisins
5ml/1 tsp - caster sugar
Little milk
Clear honey

**Method: -**
Place the mashed potato in a bowl, sift over the flour, sugar and baking powder.
Mix with a wooden spoon to form a stiff dough.
Wrap and place in the refrigerator for 30 minutes.
Peel and core the apples, cut into thin slices, cover with cold water to prevent browning while rolling out the pastry.
Roll out the pastry on a lightly floured board to cover a 20cm/8" pie dish.
Drain the apples and place in the base of the pie dish.
Sprinkle with the cinnamon, raisins and drizzle over the honey.
Use a little of the pastry to line the edge of the dish, brush with water.
Cover with the ready rolled pastry.
Cut a slit in the centre of the pastry to allow the steam to escape.
Glaze with a little milk.
Bake in the centre of a pre-heated oven, 190ºC/375ºF/gas mark 5.
Cook for 35 minutes.
Sprinkle with the sugar before serving.

## *Italian Bananas*
serves 4
*(An unusually good combination of bananas, tomatoes and onions, "Italian Bananas" is excellent with any roast meat, especially beef)*

### Ingredients: -
25g/1oz - polyunsaturated margarine
1 - onion, finely chopped
3 - tomatoes, peeled and chopped
5 - bananas, sliced
4 tbsp - dry white wine
Salt

### Method: -
Melt the margarine in a frying-pan.
Add the onion and fry until it is soft but not brown.
Add the tomatoes, bananas, wine.
Salt to taste.

## *Low Calorie Liquids*
Top up low calorie Ribena with soda water or sparkling mineral water.
Add a slice of lemon or lime to sparkling mineral water or low calorie tonic water.
Herb and fruit teas are ideal, as they need no milk and no sweetening.
A wide range of flavours are available to drink, hot or cold.
Make Indian Lassi, by mixing natural yoghurt and topping up with ice cold water.
*Green tea is high in anti-oxidants. It only needs steeping in boiling water for a short time - say 30 seconds.*

## *Low fat Christmas Pudding*

**Ingredients: -**
450g/1lb - wholemeal breadcrumbs
225/8oz - sultanas
225g/8oz - currants
100g/4oz - bananas, peeled and chopped
225g/8oz - soft brown sugar
3 - eggs
300ml/½ pint - semi skimmed milk
100g/4oz - apple, grated **not** peeled
100g/4oz - chopped Brazil nuts
30ml/2 tbsp - mixed spice
2.5ml/½ tsp salt
Juice and grated rind of 1 lemon

**Method: -**
Mix all ingredients together and stir well.
Put the mixture in a greased pudding basin and cover with greased greaseproof paper, tied on with string.
Steam the pudding for 3 hours in the normal way, allow to cool.
This pudding needs an extra 1 hour of steaming before you serve.
Turn out onto a plate. Decorate with icing sugar or a sprig of holly.
Serve with low-fat custard, or low-fat fromage frais into which you could stir 30ml/2 tbsp rum and 15ml/1 tbsp soft brown sugar. (It is not Cumberland butter, but it is much better for you).
This low fat Christmas Pudding does not keep as well as the traditional kind, but tastes just as good, if not better, and it is healthier.
This can be made just a few days before Christmas.
Makes a 1 litre/3 pint pudding or 2 x 900ml/1½ pint puddings.

## Orange Jelly Yoghurt
Serves 4

**Ingredients: -**
300ml/½ pint - unsweetened orange juice
11g/0.4oz (1 sachet) - gelatine
275g/10oz - low fat natural plain yoghurt
2 - oranges

**Method: -**
Put half of the orange juice into a saucepan and sprinkle with gelatine.
Leave the gelatine to soften for 5 minutes, then heat gently, taking care not to let it boil.
Keep stirring until all the gelatine has dissolved.
Mix together the dissolved gelatine with the remaining orange juice and yoghurt.
Pour into four serving glasses and leave to set in a cool place or refrigerator.
Cut away the peel and the pith from the oranges, cut out the orange segments and use to decorate the jelly, just before serving.
*This is also very nice with other juices and fruit, such as grapefruit juice and grapefruit segments.*

## Roasted Sunflower Seeds

**Ingredients: -**
100g/¼lb - sunflower seeds
45ml/3 tbsp - tamari sauce

**Method: -**
Heat the oven to 180º/350ºF/gas mark 4.
Put the sunflower seeds into a bowl and mix in the tamari sauce.
Spread the seeds onto a baking sheet and put them in the oven for 20 minutes.
Let the seeds cool on the baking sheet, then store them in an airtight Container.

*Nuts or seeds combined with another protein food, make a good substitute for meat or dairy products.*
*These seeds in the tamari sauce are used in salads and mixed into bread and scone dough. Good also as a before dinner snack.*
*Sunflower seeds contain vitamins D and E*

## Sunny Fruit Cocktail
serves 4 - Low-fat, high fibre

**Ingredients: -**
30ml/2 tbsp - Cointreau, Sherry, Grand Marnier or other liqueur (optional)
225g/8oz - strawberries, hulled and halved
2 large bananas - peeled and sliced
2 large peaches - halved, stoned and sliced
1 - kiwi fruit, peeled and sliced
100g/¼lb - stoned grapes
Juice of 2 oranges and 1 lemon

**Method: -**
Put the orange and lemon juice into a bowl, add the liqueur, if using.
Add the strawberries, peaches, bananas, kiwi fruit and grapes.
Fold gently into the juice.
Serve well chilled.

## Sue's Cake for Slimmers

**Ingredients: -**
450g/1lb - mixed dried fruit
1 - egg
175g/6oz - demerara sugar
225g/8oz - self raising flour
1 - cup of cold tea

**Method: -**
Mix sugar and fruit with tea and stir in beaten egg, add flour, sifted and stir well to mix.
Put in 18cm/7" cake tin and bake for 1-1½ hours at 160°C/325°F/gas mk 3.

## *Index*

Adapting Your Own Recipes   9
All about Fromage Frais   101
Amazing Sugarless Fatless Cake   102
Apple Crumble   102
Banana Cake   103
Bean & Pepper Salad   24
Bean Sprout Salad   24
Beef & Mushroom Stew with Parsley Dumplings   76
Bran & Raisin Muffins   103
Brown Rice, Lentil & Mushroom Salad   25
Bulgar Wheat Pilaff with Nuts & Seeds   78
Chicken & Garlic Casserole   78
Chicken Curry   77
Chicken with Red Wine & Tarragon   79
Chocolate Surprise Dessert   104
Cod Nicoise   65
Conversion Charts   11
Country Tomato Soup   17
Date & Walnut Bread   105
Devilled Turkey Drumsticks   80
Easy Every Day Chicken Stir-fry   81
Easy Summer Pudding   106
Eating for a Healthy Heart   9
Edna's Coconut Loaf   106
Fish Crumble   66
Five a Day   10
Fresh Orange Ring   107
Fruit Cake  (egg free) 108
Gammon Steak & Orange Sauce   82
Glazed Roast Gammon   83
Grilled chicken with Soy Sauce   84
Healthy Chicken Casserole   85
Healthy Lifestyle Pasta   13
Healthy Low fat Apple Pie   109
Healthy Seafood Lasagne   67
Herbed Fish Cakes   68
HeartCare's Aims and Objectives   7
HeartCare's Healthy Eating Hints   8
Herbs   30
Homemade Fish Stock   68
Introduction   8
Italian Bananas   110
Italian Bean Soup   18
Korean Vegetable Salad   26
Lamb with Red Capsicum Sauce   86
Lemon Sesame Chicken   87

HeartCare Healthy Lifestyle Recipes - fourth edition - 2003

## *Index (cont.)*

Lentil & Lemon Soup   19
Lettuce Soup   20
Low Calorie Liquids   110
Low Calorie/Low fat dressing   26
Low fat Christmas Pudding   111
Low fat Fish Bake   69
Low fat Vegetarian Pasta   14
Minestrone Soup   21
Mushroom Stuffed Chicken   88
Nutritional Consultancy, The   5
Orange Jelly Yoghurt   112
Orange Salad   27
Pasta & Salmon Bake   70
Petit Pois with Onions   89
Pie or Flan Case   89
Pizza   90
Poached Fish with a Lemon Sauce   71
Pork Cooked in Cider, Apples and Peppers   91
Red Cabbage Coleslaw   27
Red Peppers roasted with Cherry Tomatoes   92
Roast Potatoes with Lemon and Rosemary   92
Roasted Sunflower Seeds   112
Salmon Steaks in Mushroom Sauce   72
Savoury Jacket Potatoes   93
Smoked Mackerel Pâté   15
Southern non-Fried Chicken   93
Spiced Lamb & Beef Risotto   94
Spices   42
Stuffed Red Peppers   95
Sue's Cake for Slimmers   113
Summer Trout in Foil   73
Sunny Fruit Cocktail   113
Sweet & Sour Turkey   96
Tomato & Basil Soup   22
Tuna Pasta & Broccoli Bake   74
Tuna Pâté   15
Vegetable Curry   97
Vegetable Pilaf   98
Vegetarian Nut Roast   98
Vinaigrette (French Dressing)   27
Vitamin Table   10
Wholemeal Asparagus or Vegetable Flan   99
Wild Rice & Asparagus Salad   27